Previous Titles:

Free to Be Human — Intellectual Self-Defence in an Age of Illusions, Green Books, 1995. ISBN:1870098889

The Compassionate Revolution — Radical Politics and Buddhism, Green Books, 1998. ISBN:1870098706

Guardians of Power — The Myth of the Liberal Media (with David Cromwell), Pluto Press, 2006. ISBN: 0745324827

Newspeak in the 21st Century (with David Cromwell), Pluto Press, 2009. 0745328938

Propaganda Blitz — How the Corporate Media Distort Reality (with David Cromwell), Pluto Press, 2018. ISBN: 978 0 7453 3811 8

What People Are Saying About

A Short Book About Ego…

I have learnt a great deal reading *A Short Book About Ego,* a thoughtful and gentle book about the change of consciousness we all need to go through. I read it just after reading the *Bhagavad Gita* while travelling through northern Pakistan, which gave me extra context.
Peter Oborne, award-winning journalist and broadcaster, author of *The Fate of Abraham: Why the West Is Wrong About Islam*

The best way to transcend the ego is to understand it. This book shines a bright light on the machinations of the ego, and shows us a glimpse of freedom beyond it. Best of all, it highlights the clearest path to freedom, through the practice of meditation.
Steve Taylor, PhD, author of *The Leap* and *Extraordinary Awakenings*

David Edwards shoots straight from the heart at the brilliant stupidity of head-trapped humans and our knack for needless suffering. This book is a creative and witty guide for how to live with sanity and joy in a world that rarely makes it easy. David offers the reader a diagnosis and a remedy and leaves the rest to us. It's an incisive deconstruction of human delusion. And an opportunity to ponder on the great matters of love and freedom.
Richard Gilpin, psychotherapist and author of *Mindfulness for Unravelling Anxiety — Finding Calm & Clarity in Uncertain Times*

A Short Book About Ego is a brilliant and concise call to arms. It shows us that those of us who wish to transform the chaos of the world we see everywhere around us must first learn to transform ourselves inwardly. Our ego is our enemy, the self an illusion (standing at the centre of a circle of mirrors), and the road to freedom lies in inner stillness and learning the ancient art of meditation. David Edwards is one of the most important writers at work today. In a saner and more emotionally wise society, he would be both a household name and a national treasure.
Torben Betts, award-winning UK playwright and author of *Invincible, Muswell Hill* and *Murder in the Dark*

I am a huge admirer of David's work at Media Lens. Media Lens is one of very, very few news sources that seek to present news stories without bias. Rather than doing the journalism that pays, they have chosen to take the difficult path and write with integrity and present the uncomfortable truths that corporate media choose to ignore. I'm so grateful for their work. It must be very difficult to be so committed to do this work day-in and day-out and continue, unwaveringly, over decades. I often wondered how they managed to do it without being driven to despair and frustration. As David shows in this book, he uses meditation to help provide a shield and source of inspiration to do this difficult work. He argues that this practice gives us all the strength to act decisively and independently. By reaching within, we can free ourselves. And he makes a very compelling argument that there has been a systematic effort to try to undermine this refuge so that we are more likely to go along with the propaganda and advertising messages by which we are bombarded every day. I highly recommend this book.
Chris Haughton, author and illustrator of *A Bit Lost* and the forthcoming *The History of Information*

A Short Book About Ego … and the Remedy of Meditation

David Edwards

A Short Book About Ego … and the Remedy of Meditation

David Edwards

London, UK
Washington, DC, USA

First published by Mantra Books, 2025
Mantra Books is an imprint of Collective Ink Ltd.,
Unit 11, Shepperton House, 89 Shepperton Road, London, N1 3DF
office@collectiveinkbooks.com
www.collectiveinkbooks.com
www.mantra-books.net

For distributor details and how to order please visit the 'Ordering' section on our website.

ISBN: 978 1 80341 816 2
978 1 80341 869 8 (ebook)
Library of Congress Control Number: 2024937849

A CIP catalogue record for this book is available from the British Library.

Design: Lapiz Digital Services

UK: Printed and bound by CPI Group (UK) Ltd, Croydon, CR0 4YY
Printed in North America by CPI GPS partners

'Unusual though it is in this decadent age
I offer these words without treachery, so
listen well.'
— Patrul Rinpoche, nineteenth-century Buddhist teacher

For Sonia with love

Contents

Chapter 1: The Successful, Suffering and Righteous Egos 1
The Incredible Shrinking Springsteen 4
'Every Time a Friend Succeeds...' 6
The Suffering Ego 10
The Righteous Ego — A Different Kind of 'Special One' 14
'You Think It's Funny Turning Rebellion into Money?' 17
Where Egos Dare — 'Do You Know Who I Am?' 20
Ego — The Root of All Prejudice 22
Chapter 2: Meditation — The Remedy 27
Midnight Thought Storm 29
'Face It. Feel It Fully' 31
Internal Flowers — The Big Surprise 32
The 'Divine Melody' 36
The Unsinkable Heart 39
Too Good to Be True? 42
Hector the Helicopter's Dream 45
Chapter 3: Transforming Suffering into Love and Bliss 49
Removing the Splinter 49
Ballad of the 'Broken-Hearted' Ego 56
'I Like You, but I Don't Love You...' 58
Jumping into the Tiger's Mouth 60
The Art of Do-It-Yourself Ultimate Romance 63
Imprisoned in Bliss 64
Desire: 'Something to Yield To or Be Overcome?' 69
Keeping Company with Desire 72

Chapter 4: Misdirected — Looking in the Wrong Direction 78
Misdirected 1 — The Failure of External 'Success' 81
Misdirected 2 — Head-Trapped Intellectuals 93
Brain in a Jar — The Break Out! 100
Jean-Jacques Rousseau — The Man with No Skin 108
Epilogue: 'Burning Among Stars in the Night' 110
Note from the Author 120
Bibliography 121

Chapter 1

The Successful, Suffering and Righteous Egos

The human mind stands at the centre of a circle of mirrors.

The mirrors — parents, friends, lovers, teachers, strangers — constantly reflect images of who we are. We're told we're annoying, adorable, stupid, unlovable; that we're a show-off, that we're not academic, that we've got a nice voice, that we're a fast runner, dance beautifully, and so on.

The reflections collect as a nebulous mass in which we perceive an indistinct outline of an individual, a personality, a self — 'me'. This is the ego, the mind identifying itself with impressions from the outside world.

But how is this possible? How can we shape a solid sense of self out of a chaos of reflected impressions? The answer is that the mind has an astonishing capacity to identify with almost anything.

The body, of course, is 'mine' — if someone mocks my shape, colour or size, they mock 'me'. But beliefs are also 'mine' — if someone attacks 'my' religion, 'my' politics, 'my' country's flag, I may also react as if they had attacked 'me'.

I identify with 'my' job. Who am I? I'm a writer, a doctor, a scientist, a plumber. In the morning, a businessman or woman puts on a suit which, for the ego, becomes a kind of second skin, a part of the self. It tells us we are an 'executive', perhaps a 'manager' or 'managing director'; we are 'white collar' or 'blue collar'.

Leaving the house, we put on a car — a metal suit, a metal skin. If we're driving a Jaguar, we know we're prowling near the top of the motoring food chain. We feel the power of the engine as our own, we share the status of the brand. We roar away from the Mini at the traffic lights with the same sense of superiority felt by the bodybuilder for the bespectacled nerd.

Arriving at our workplace, we take off our car and put on our office; our egos instantly absorbing any prestige associated with our job title, department, company brand, which all become part of the composite self. BBC journalist and former editor of the *Independent* newspaper, Andrew Marr, wrote:

> To be a national newspaper editor is a grand thing. Even at the poor-mouse *Independent*, though I didn't have a chauffeur, I was driven to and from work in a limousine, barking orders down my mobile phone. In the office, I was the commander.
>
> Eyes swivelled when I arrived and people at least pretended to listen when I spoke. The Indy might be small, but she was *mine*.[1]

Actually, 'she' was not just 'mine'; 'she' was '*me*'.

Arriving home at the end of the day, we take off our office, car and suit, and put on our house or flat. Property is a crucial mirror reflecting our status back at us. An Englishman does not just view his home as his castle; he views his 'castle' as an extension of himself.

Anyone visiting Propertied Man or Woman will find themselves in the presence of a well-appointed, detached or semi-detached ego; one that may be polite and generous, but which will be very much in charge of what happens in 'my' castle-suit, in 'my' house-skin. Comments of this kind are heard:

> I won't be spoken to like that in my own house.

And:

> Sorry – my house, my rules.

In visiting other people, we take off our own property suit, shrink to human size and, in a sometimes dramatic and observable change, meekly defer to other Property People — especially towering, Downton Abbey-sized giants.

For more than 25 years when I visited my parents' bungalow in Kent, I used to top up the water in their small, neglected goldfish pond. I'd pull out weeds, tighten the anti-heron netting, drop in some orange fish flakes. As old age took hold of my father, he became a mostly silent, owl-like presence perched on the end of the sofa looking for things to criticise. Once, in a dry spell, he noticed I'd reeled the hose out to give the pond a much-needed top-up. From the sofa, he looked at me severely as I entered the lounge:

> Are you putting more water in the pond?
> Yes.
> Well, turn it off.
> Why?
> It costs me a lot of money.

Taking a leaf from Gandhi's *satyagraha* strategy of non-violent resistance, I replied:

> No problem, I'm happy to pay for it. How much do you want?
> Twenty pounds!

I quickly held out a twenty-pound note, which my father gruffly trousered and, as quickly, un-trousered following a humanitarian intervention from my mother. As I left the room, I heard him say:

> That bugger defies me in my own house!

The Incredible Shrinking Springsteen

It makes sense that a self composed of reflected opinions will be insecure, transient, a trembling mass of contradictions. No matter how 'superior' and exalted, the ego is always anxious. The circling mirrors may spin a splendid image of a 'successful' self, but it can never be more than an illusion. It is no more substantial than a rainbow; there is no solid ground on which to stand.

This is why even the most 'famous' and 'successful' among us are bewildered by the fact that they can be confident to the point of arrogance and yet haunted by self-doubt.

A striking example was provided when rock legend, Bruce Springsteen, described his reaction to former US President Barack Obama's suggestion that they do a podcast together:

> ...my first thought was: 'OK, I'm a high school graduate from Freehold, New Jersey, who plays the guitar ... What's wrong with this picture?' My wife Patti said: 'Are you insane?! Do it! People would love to hear your conversations!'[2]

Faced by the even more famous and powerful Obama, one of the most successful, highly respected rock 'stars' of our time shrank to the size of a lowly high-school student. Springsteen, himself known as 'The Boss', added of Obama:

> He'll go out of his way to make you feel comfortable, as he did for me *so that I might have the confidence to sit across the table from him.*[3]

As this suggests, there is always somebody around the corner who is 'superior' in some way, who has even more attention credits. And while the world may have reflected 'beautiful', 'talented', 'young', 'beloved' back at us yesterday, what about today?

So the ego must forever seek out more positive reflections, more attention. Without them, the self-image starts to dissolve. As yesterday's reflections fade, the feeling grows that we are becoming colourless, insubstantial. If this continues long enough, we start to feel like a 'has-been', a ghost, a 'nobody'. It is a feeling highlighted, of course, by the presence of 'somebodies'.

Wherever children are playing, we inevitably hear the ego's mantra:

Look mummy! Look at me! Look daddy!

We can never have enough attention and this quickly becomes the dominant theme of our lives.

We seek 'fame' but we're actually seeking attention. We seek wealth but we're seeking attention. We seek to 'express ourselves' on Twitter/X, Facebook, Instagram and TikTok, but we're seeking attention. We seek political power but we're seeking attention, attention, attention. We seek to 'save the world', but we're seeking attention. We want our circle of mirrors to be packed with applauding admirers. We don't much care about their motivation, or ours.

As we will see in Chapter 3, what we call 'romantic love' is often a two-way flood of ultra-positive reflections boosting self-image. 'You're so easy to talk to, I feel like I've known you all my life. I've never felt this way about anyone before, I can't stop thinking about you.'

When this flow of positive attention is suddenly reduced — or, worse, diverted towards someone else deemed even more 'special' — we are tortured.

When the torrent of parental attention lavished on a toddling girl suddenly diverts to a bouncing baby sibling, the girl's emerging ego is bereft. For the rest of her life, she may give attention to her younger rival through gritted teeth, especially in the presence of her parents. Any good qualities he or she might have will become negatives in her mind precisely because they earn them *yet more* stolen attention! Deep into middle-age and beyond, they may forever be viewed as a selfish, attention-seeking little parasite of parental love.

'Every Time a Friend Succeeds...'

We are told: 'Smile and the world smiles with you, cry and you cry alone.'

It's not quite true. In fact, it's sobering to examine how we *really* feel when confronted by the good fortune of others. Despite perhaps being genuinely pleased on one level — we care about them, we're happy that they're happy — our egos feel awkward, uneasy, marginalised. We find ourselves guiltily swatting away those three little words that seem to be spoken by a grisly inner 5-year-old; words that we hardly dare express, even to ourselves: *What about me?!*

We supply the obligatory congratulations, of course, but our eyes fail to match the smiles on lips that quickly crumble at the edges. We are not enjoying the fact that their success makes our lives seem humdrum by comparison. We sit cold-eyed, grinning a little too fiercely, as they tell us about their lottery win, their new 'celebrity' friends, the incredible adventures on their round-the-world trip. The conflict and pretence are exhausting. Later, revenge will be exacted:

> Can you believe it? She's just won the lottery and didn't buy a single round of drinks!

Or:

> Did you see him splashing his lottery money around the pub like he owned the place? Flash git!

As novelist and wit Gore Vidal said:

> Every time a friend succeeds, I die a little.[4]

If we are tempted to dismiss Vidal as a cynical modern, consider this observation regarding seventeenth-century Zen master Bankei:

> After Bankei had passed away, a blind man who lived near the master's temple said to a friend:
>
> 'Since I am blind I cannot watch a person's face, so I must judge his character by the sound of his voice. Ordinarily when I hear someone congratulate another upon his happiness or success, I also hear a secret tone of envy. When condolence is expressed for the misfortune of another, I hear pleasure and satisfaction, as if the one condoling was really glad there was something left to gain in his own world.
>
> 'In all my experience however, Bankei's voice was always sincere. Whenever he expressed happiness, I heard nothing but happiness, and whenever he expressed sorrow, sorrow was all I heard.'[5]

Closer to our own time, tennis 'star' John McEnroe described life back home after his first, unexpected success at Wimbledon:

> ...from the moment I got back, the people I had grown up with wouldn't let me feel the same, or so I thought. Suddenly I was Somebody, while they were still nobodies... My friends weren't quite sure how to handle it and neither was I.[6]

No surprise, then, that 'celebrities' try hard to emphasise their humility. They know that fame and fortune generate a store of public resentment that can easily explode. It's child's play for our egos to rationalise turning on 'stars' who are 'over-rated', 'over the top', 'over the hill'. Whenever a 'star' is praised, our alarmed egos reflexively look for counter-arguments.

Why are gossip magazines and TV programmes so vicious about 'celebrities', and why do people love to read and watch them? Because 'stars' sail far 'above' us in the attentional firmament — they get the public interest and 'high life' we crave and deserve. Down here, 'unknown', our egos quietly plot revenge.

In *The Guardian*, John Harris observed that Philip Norman's best-selling biography of The Beatles' *Shout!* contained an ugly flaw:

> ...a glaring bias against Paul McCartney, who was portrayed as a kind of simpering egomaniac, and a correspondingly overgenerous view of Lennon, who, Norman later claimed, represented 'three quarters of The Beatles'.[7]

Norman later confessed that his damning view of McCartney 'was a reaction to how much he [Norman] had once not just admired him, but wanted to somehow be up there, in his place'.

With admirable honesty, Norman said:

> If I'm honest, all those years I'd spent wishing to be him had left me feeling in some obscure way that I needed to get my own back.[8]

Robert Pirsig, author of *Zen and the Art of Motorcycle Maintenance*, said of his fans:

> They love you for being what they all want to be, but they hate you for being what they are not.[9]

The hate is real. It's no surprise that when people deemed 'somebodies' are attacked and even murdered, it's quite often by people tormented by the (baseless) conviction that they are 'nobodies'.

Norman underestimated the extent of the problem; even if he had not wanted *to be* McCartney, the admiration he felt would have been sufficient to provoke his ego to seek revenge. Whenever we admire someone, our ego is painfully aware that it is looking 'up'. That humiliation must be put right, corrected.

If we die a little when others succeed, we thrive a little when others fail, supplying a balm to our ego's wounds. There is a subtle relief that we are not enduring the same problem – we feel newly alert to the comfort and security of our lives. We are happy to offer help because doing so indicates that our life situation is preferable in this moment – a welcome boost to our self-esteem.

This accounts for the extraordinary fact that people so often hate to be offered advice or help which, however useful, obliges the recipient's ego to accept that it temporarily holds an 'inferior' position. After all, he is claiming to know something we don't; she thinks she's more in the know – wiser, more experienced – on this particular issue. Our ego becomes anxious, looks for a way to restore parity.

An astonishing number of arguments and feuds has its origin in the offering and rejection of advice. Parents are particularly annoyed by their children's advice: 'I wiped his bum as a kid, now he's telling me how to live my life!'

This reaction, in turn, of course, is deeply offensive to the child's ego – advice is being rejected precisely *because* he or she is still seen as 'lower', as 'just a child'. We may feel uneasy even when someone recommends a film or book:

> You *have* to read this!
> Oh, *do* I?!

The implication: they have discovered something important that we don't know about. Our ego gets twitchy. Do they think they're better-read? If someone lends a 'serious' novel to a kidult fan of Harry Potter, the kidult's ego will sizzle as they scour the 'serious' reader's face for the tiniest sign of superiority indicating she is a missionary come to elevate our literary tastes. If in doubt, just in case, the ego will take revenge. This may manifest as a physical inability to pick the book up. If the book has been written by the giver – writers order piles of extra copies to selflessly donate to friends, family and any other victims they can find – it will take a Herculean effort for the recipient to even get past the front cover. If the giver is a literary or political ally – i.e. a competitor – the book will likely go straight up onto a shelf, or be thrown like a frisbee to the back of a cupboard:

> Fascinating, no doubt, but I've read what he has to say a *hundred* times!

Solidarity, brother!

The Suffering Ego

The ego's difficulty with the happiness of others is relentlessly communicated to children.

Adults stoically tolerate youthful exuberance for a while – their happiness is our priority, right? But the glee soon starts to grate. Our auditory senses become excruciatingly acute as we focus on 'the racket' – the laughter, giggles and screams of delight – although the real racket is the one being made by the ego between our ears:

> For God's sake pipe down, I'm trying to read my newspaper! Stop showing off! Go outside and play. Will you calm down before you hurt yourself!

Although children are bewildered to receive such hostility for being joyful, the message is clear: curb your enthusiasm.

An octogenarian relative once confessed to me that he felt bitterly jealous of the young — they're bursting with energy, falling in and out of love, able to run and dance, parties every night. How could he not reflect that his excitement consisted of the daily run to Tesco, worrying about when to put the bins out, and watching the News five times a day? 'Young people today!' The real problem — today, yesterday and every day — is that old people were young once and are no longer. Schopenhauer put it bluntly:

> The fundamental difference between youth and age will always be that the former has in prospect life, the latter death.[10]

Children are a spotlight illuminating our jaded *joie de vivre*, our age-related grumpiness. Finding fault with youthful joy soothes the ego's pain; they may have everything we have lost, but their 'lack of responsibility and consideration for others' is 'intolerable'.

The deeper problem with all of this is that the young may learn that they are treated far better when they are *not* happy. When sad or ill, they instantly become the centre of attention; the carping is replaced by kindness and concern. They're told to lie down and take it easy; everything is done for them.

The attention-hungry ego quickly learns that declarations of suffering are a prime way of winning positive regard. Indeed, 'I feel awful!' makes us the focus of attention in a way unmatched even by exam, sports and career success. After all, our suffering does not provoke a jealous parental backlash.

The parents of 1970s global teen pop sensation, David Cassidy, were both in show business. Alas, the greatest claim to fame of Cassidy's father, Jack, was being bumped off by Clint

Eastwood in *The Eiger Sanction*. With rare candour, Cassidy junior wrote:

> My parents wanted success for themselves so desperately that they couldn't be happy for me ... my fame became torture for my mother as well as my father.[11]

Children learn the fateful lesson that, if they are sufficiently sad or ill, the universe, in the form of their parents, will intervene to save them. Many take this lesson into adulthood, with grim consequences.

We might imagine that a person apparently, or actually, beset with problems bears no relation to the stereotypical tycoon puffing on a large cigar in the back of a Rolls. But, in fact, our egos can learn to use suffering to make themselves the centre of attention, to justify domineering behaviour, in much the same way. Arguably, this Suffering Ego is an even more insidious form of egotism because it doesn't *look* like egotism. This makes it difficult to challenge — we fear we are being brutal, unkind, that any criticism may prove the last straw.

In his short story, *Louise,* Somerset Maugham describes the eponymous character as someone who appears to use a heart complaint — which may or may not be quite as serious as claimed — to dominate and control the people around her. Louise marries Tom Maitland who is young, healthy and rich. With typically wicked, sardonic humour, Maugham wrote:

> Tom Maitland was a big, husky fellow, very good-looking and a fine athlete. He doted on Louise. With her weak heart he could not hope to keep her with him long and he made up his mind to do everything he could to make her few years on earth happy. He gave up the games he excelled in, not because she wished him to, she was glad that he should play golf and hunt, but because by a

> coincidence she had a heart attack whenever he proposed to leave her for a day. If they had a difference of opinion, she gave in to him at once, for she was the most submissive wife a man could have, but her heart failed her and she would be laid up, sweet and uncomplaining, for a week. He could not be such a brute as to cross her. Then they would have quite a little tussle about which should yield and it was only with difficulty that at last he persuaded her to have her own way.[12]

Finally, Louise is confronted by the sceptical narrator, an old friend:

> I suppose it's never struck you as strange that you're always strong enough to do anything you want to and that your weak heart only prevents you from doing things that bore you?[13]

Not all Suffering Egos are such control freaks. It may simply be understood that the focus of the conversation should be on *their* 'special' problems and suffering – these are the ones that really matter. The immense weight of the cross they bear is such that their behaviour should be judged by different standards. We must work hard to help *them*, but who would be so heartless as to suggest reciprocation?

Because the Suffering Ego generates attention and dominance from its misery – exactly as the Successful Ego does from wealth and fame – it has a big investment in continuing to appear miserable to the outside world. Laura Archera Huxley wrote:

> There is a widespread though subterranean feeling that to be made to suffer – to be a victim – is somehow an admirable position on earth and a good ticket to a special place in heaven.[14]

But it is surely *not* an admirable position because, as Huxley asked:

> When do I do the most good for myself and for others:
> When I am suffering –
> Or when I am happy?

The investment in suffering explains the otherwise bewildering phenomenon whereby the Suffering Ego contemptuously, even angrily, dismisses all proposed solutions. Why? Because solutions threaten the whole basis of the Suffering Ego, much as bankruptcy threatens the ego of a billionaire. Indeed, a clear sign of the presence of a Suffering Ego is precisely this hostile reaction to possible solutions, impatiently dismissed as an additional, intolerable burden:

> What on earth do you know about it? You can't possibly understand what I'm going through.

The Righteous Ego — A Different Kind of 'Special One'

The Successful Ego, of course, raises itself above others on its 'special' achievements. Football manager, José Mourinho, enraged egos everywhere by saying:

> Please don't call me arrogant, but I'm European champion and I think I'm a special one.[15]

Sports journalists have never forgiven Mourinho for this comment and love to remind him and us of it every time he's sacked by a club: 'Is Mourinho *still* "the special one"?' The journalistic ego deeply resents being a mere commentator on the lives of 'stars' hogging the limelight, just as editors and publishers resent being 'mere' facilitators of their authors' work.

While the Suffering Ego raises itself up on its own 'special' problems, the Righteous Ego's 'specialness' lies in its unusual concern for the problems of *others*. The comedy series, *Seinfeld*, loved to nail this form of pride. After an uncharacteristically selfless act of generosity, Jerry thinks to himself:

> I am such a great guy! Who else would've gone through the trouble of helping this poor immigrant? I *am* special. My mother was right.[16]

Torben Betts has been described as 'An uncommonly gifted playwright' (*Time Out*) and 'a political Beckett'. In his 2012 play, *Muswell Hill*, Betts' character, Julian, is a fine example of a Righteous Ego. Julian's widow, Karen, reveals that her tormented husband had committed suicide by throwing himself off the cliff at Beachy Head:

> Sometimes he could be a right moody old sod, but I understood him, you see... Because he was such a strict vegetarian, he ended up despising all meat eaters and because he was such a committed cyclist he hated all motorists. And he'd get so wound up by people's indifference and stupidity that he used to be so full of ... well, hatred.[17]

It is not a small thing to rail at the lack of compassion in the people around us; it means that they are all morally 'inferior'. On this basis, our ego will feel entitled to rage, preach and patronise — to assert its dominance over *everyone* — as brutally as any Successful Ego or Suffering Ego. It ought to be a thing of wonder that so many people ostensibly motivated by compassion for human and animal suffering, are 'full of ... well, hatred'.

The complexity lies in the fact that we can be absolutely right – human beings *are* often indifferent, the social system *is* structurally unjust, Western foreign policy *is* rooted in medieval-style greed and violence, and our egos *can* hijack being right to justify our own tyrannical abuse.

Others may be wealthier, more famous and beautiful, but the Righteous Ego can slip the surly bonds of 'ordinariness' and ascend to the moral 'high ground'. If we have a political argument with someone we perceive as more conventionally successful (a parent, for example), our Righteous Ego may fight tooth and nail to establish our 'superiority' in at least this 'ethical' dimension.

In short, if the billionaire's Successful Ego feels 'superior' because it has more financial credit, the Righteous Ego feels 'superior' because it has more moral credit.

Small gestures will do. Having spent decades working for a climate-killing oil company, or an international bank, we can point to our vegan diet, our meticulous recycling, or the fact that we read the supposedly left-liberal *The Guardian* newspaper as proof that we are nevertheless more 'ethical' than others. The flimsier the support for the Righteous Ego, the more fiercely that support will be defended. Even polite, rational questioning of the health benefits of veganism, or the left credentials of *The Guardian*, may set the fur flying.

A key problem is that the extreme, domineering behaviour of a Righteous Ego can easily be mistaken for extreme compassion – they're angry, impatient and abusive *because* they care so much. In reality, predatory individuals and organisations have always understood that they can hide their crimes behind a screen of fake compassion. British readers will recall how, for 20 years, the BBC's serial child rapist and abuser, Jimmy Savile, presented a TV programme ostensibly dedicated to fulfilling the dreams of children: 'Jim'll Fix It'. Tony Blair, who oversaw the

Iraq oil grab costing at least one million Iraqi lives, made much of his party's 'ethical foreign policy'. The Italian philosopher, Machiavelli, wrote:

> It is not essential ... that a Prince should have all the good qualities which I have enumerated above, but it is most essential that *he should seem to have them* ... Thus, it is well to *seem* merciful, faithful, humane, religious and upright, and also to be so; but the mind should remain so balanced that were it needful to be so, you should be able and know how to change to the contrary.[18]

The crucial word here, repeated twice: *seem*. What looks like concern may just be cover for a domineering ego. This frequently becomes obvious when The Righteous Ego is offered a choice between remaining 'merciful, faithful, humane' and winning 'mainstream success'.

'You Think It's Funny Turning Rebellion into Money?'

Righteous Egos pursuing political change, for example, are highly vulnerable to the temptation of transitioning to more standard Successful Egos. Time and again, I have seen young, idealistic writers start out on radical websites, only to succumb to the lure, not just of joining the 'mainstream' corporate press, but of doing so by self-censoring and compromising their message. I've seen wonderfully unique, clear-thinking voices mangled by their struggle to sew with a double-pointed needle – telling the truth while being accepted, embraced and rewarded by a heavily filtered media system.

We see this tendency throughout modern culture. Consider The Clash, one of the fiercest anti-establishment, anti-capitalist bands of the punk era. Their song, *London Calling* (1979) was an apocalyptic call to arms. The title mocked the BBC World

Service's tradition of beginning its reports 'This is London calling...', much as the Sex Pistols' song, *God Save The Queen*, mocked the UK's (then) *de facto* national anthem. The website *Songfacts* says of *London Calling*:

> It was the song that best defined The Clash, who were known for lashing out against injustice and rebelling against the establishment, which is pretty much what punk rock was all about.[19]

In photo shoots, The Clash were often depicted as a menacing, grim-faced street gang in black leather jackets, Doc Martin boots and 'bondage' trousers (music magazines used to sell this 'Clash gear' to fans). The call from London was for popular insurrection:

> London calling to the faraway towns, now that war is declared and battle come down.[20]

In the early 1990s, The Clash resisted a request from British Telecom to use *London Calling* in an advert. But by 2002, singer-songwriter Joe Strummer had sold the rights to the song to luxury car manufacturer Jaguar for use in an advert. Strummer explained:

> Yeah. I agreed to that. We get hundreds of requests for that and turn 'em all down. But I just thought Jaguar ... yeah. If you're in a group and you make it together, then everybody deserves something. Especially twenty-odd years after the fact. It just seems churlish for a writer to refuse to have their music used on an advert...[21]

'Churlish' or not, in the 1978 Clash hit, *(White Man) In Hammersmith Palais*, Strummer had sung:

> The new groups are not concerned
> With what there is to be learned
> They got Burton suits.
> Ha, you think it's funny
> Turning rebellion into money?[22]

London Calling was used in an advert for the Jaguar X-Type – 'a sleek four-door aimed at the "entry-level luxury" segment and retailing for a relatively modest $30,000'.[23]

The song was later used in a 2012 British Airways advert and in the James Bond movie *Die Another Day*. At one point, Strummer actually worked as a DJ for the BBC World Service on a programme called 'Joe Strummer's London Calling'. After the band broke up, another Clash song, *Should I Stay Or Should I Go*, made it to number 1 in the UK, heavily assisted by its inclusion in a Levi jeans advert. *The Boston Globe* commented:

> By now you could make a pretty good compilation of subversive music that's been used in ads, with selections from Lou Reed (*Perfect Day* in a spot for the NFL), Iggy Pop (both *Lust for Life* in a Carnival Cruises ad, and the Stooges song *Search & Destroy* in a Nike commercial for the 1996 Olympics), the Ramones (Bud Light once used *Blitzkrieg Bop*), the Buzzcocks (Toyota), and even Creedence Clearwater Revival's scathing indictment of America's privileged class, *Fortunate Son* (repurposed by Wrangler) ... The famously lefty British band Chumbawumba sold the rights to the song *Pass It Along* ... to Pontiac, and then turned their earnings over to a progressive activist network.[24]

The Sex Pistols were a major inspiration for The Clash. Tragicomically, the Pistols' singer, Johnny Rotten, later dressed up as a country squire in a commercial selling Country Life butter.[25]

Where Egos Dare — 'Do You Know Who I Am?'

In my work as a writer, I've met and interacted online with a lot of 'celebrity' journalists, academics, activists, diplomats and businesspeople. A common trait, I find, is that they subtly, or not so subtly, demand deference. This is to be expressed through exaggerated interest and respect. It must be clear that we feel thrilled and honoured to be in their company. We are to make their opinions and lives the central focus of the conversation, to let them dominate.

If we contribute an anecdote from our own lives, we must be careful to play it down: 'In my own small way, I've ... I'm not comparing my experience with yours, obviously, but ...'

Our conditioning is such that it is actually quite difficult to accept that 'ordinary' and 'celebrity' humans are of equal importance. However unlikely that sounds when considering the likes of Elvis, Marilyn Monroe and The King, imagine arguing that the suffering of a 'star' was more important than that of any 'ordinary' person. The idea is actually monstrous, absurd.

The required behaviour in the presence of a 'celebrity' is not dissimilar from the way we are expected to cringe and cower before kings and queens. Quite obviously, to bow and curtsy is to literally signal that we are 'lower' and they 'higher'.

TV presenter Joan Bakewell, who had an affair with Nobel Prize-winning playwright, Harold Pinter, for eight years, wrote:

> Harold had always dispatched manuscript copies of his plays to a small group of his closest friends. We knew to respond as soon as possible to acknowledge, congratulate and enthuse about the play; given their dazzling quality, it wasn't hard to do.[26]

Bakewell added:

> Harold was deeply needful of support from those he trusted. More than that, he could fly into a wild temper if their response was not forthcoming.
>
> He grew to be like that with people. There are accounts of his explosive anger in public that grew more frequent as he took up political causes. His friends knew to fear and avoid the volcanic temper.

To remain in the company of a 'celebrity' is often conditional on accepting an unspoken inequality. If we unthinkingly start treating them like 'ordinary' people, we will be sharply reminded of who we are talking to.

Indeed, the question forever hovering at the back of the 'celebrity' mind: 'Do you know who I am?' Thus, on being arrested for a traffic offence, U2's guitarist, the Edge, repeatedly shouted at police:

> I am the Edge![27]

When cabin crew attempted to prevent REM's guitarist, Peter Buck, from creating mayhem on a flight, he shouted:

> I am REM and I can have you arrested![28]

My own feeling is that future generations — more realistically, other life forms on distant planets not subject to runaway climate change — will view people standing on a stage in front of tens of thousands of people as peak egotistical pathology.

In conversation with people like the Edge and Buck, it is understood that our concerns are less important — our interest in their issues need not be reciprocated. I should add, by the way, that I have also met 'celebrities' who are not like this. These are people who understand the game and don't like to cause suffering and humiliation to others.

Ego — The Root of All Prejudice

It is not difficult to appreciate that sexism, racism, classism and speciesism are all manifestations of ego.

One can feel 'superior' because one is a human, a millionaire, a PhD, a vegan, a Greenpeace activist, or afflicted by terrible suffering. And we can, of course, feel 'special' on the basis of gender, religion and race. It is a remarkable feature of the ego that it can perceive itself as fundamentally 'superior' to others on the basis of differences that are literally skin deep. The self-serving bias is often laughably transparent. Thus, the renowned Swedish botanist, zoologist and taxonomist, Carl Linnaeus, wrote:

> The [Native] American is obstinate, contented, free; the European, mobile, keen, inventive; the Asiatic cruel, splendour-loving, miserly; the African sly, lazy, indifferent. The American is covered with tattooing, and rules by habit; the European is covered with close-fitting garments and rules by law; the Asiatic is enclosed in flowing garments and rules by opinion; the African is anointed with grease and rules by whim.[29]

Happily, then, it is Linnaeus's own type, the European, that turns out to be keen, inventive, well-dressed and law-abiding, while the rest are obstinate, cruel, miserly, sly, lazy, indifferent and lawless.

One hundred years ago, the anarchist social critic Rudolf Rocker quoted the extreme loathing of nineteenth-century German intellectuals for the French:

> Hatred of the foreigner, hatred of the French, of their trifling, their vanity, their folly, their language, their customs; yes, burning hatred of all that comes from them,

> that must unite everything German firmly and fraternally; and German valour, German freedom, German culture, German honour and justice must again soar high and be raised to the old honour and glory whereby our fathers shone before most of the peoples of the earth.[30]

And:

> It comes to the same thing if one teaches his daughters French or trains them for whores.[31]

Germans are not considered a separate race from the French, but these comments are as dehumanising and hate filled as more familiar forms of prejudice. It is clear that large numbers of German egos were identifying with the abstract label 'German', and making themselves 'special', 'higher' than the French and other 'foreigners'.

Responses to sexism and racism tend to focus on angry denunciations, and above all on demands that 'hate speech' should be circumscribed, deleted, even made illegal. But censorship and legal prohibitions do little to address the root cause: the ego's deep need to be 'special', 'superior'. Even if we completely censor one form of prejudice, the ego will find some other way to 'rise above'.

We can rearrange the deckchairs on our Titanic egos if we like – apply a little 'Me Too' awareness here, some Black Lives Matter concern there. But until the discussion turns to the issue of egotism – how the ego's circle of mirrors generates a sense of self, why this 'image' is inherently insecure, why it causes us to endlessly compete for 'special' attention confirming our status as a 'star', as *herrenvolk*, as people worthy of 'American exceptionalism' – then we will continue ploughing through oceans teeming with prejudicial icebergs.

The problem is not merely what we say, do, or believe about different genders and races; it is about *the fundamental nature of the ego.*

Only when the issue of ego makes it onto the agenda can we begin to understand the key importance of the only antidote ever found with the power to dissolve the ego and its bias. In the chapters that follow, we will discuss how that antidote is awareness, introspection, watching, witnessing — the great remedy of meditation.

1. Andrew Marr, *My Trade — A Short History of British Journalism*, Macmillan, 2004, pp.190–191; my emphasis.
2. Bruce Springsteen and Barack Obama, 'Springsteen and Obama on friendship and fathers: "You have to turn your ghosts into ancestors"' in *The Guardian*, 23 October 2021. https://www.theguardian.com/culture/2021/oct/23/bruce-springsteen-and-barack-obama-on-friendship-and-fathers-book-renegades.
3. Ibid., my emphasis.
4. Stuart Jeffries and Stephen Moss, 'The A-Z of Gore Vidal' in *The Guardian*, 1 August 2012. https://www.theguardian.com/books/2012/aug/01/the-a-z-gore-vidal.
5. Bankei, quoted, Osho, *Dang Dang Doko Dang*, Osho Media International, 2015, p.30.
6. John McEnroe, *Serious*, Hachette Digital, 2008, p.64.
7. John Harris, 'Paul McCartney by Philip Norman review — the Beatle finally gets his due' in *The Guardian*, 28 May 2016; my emphasis. https://www.theguardian.com/books/2016/may/28/paul-mccartney-the-biography-by-philip-norman-review.
8. Norman, cited, ibid.
9. Pirsig, quoted, Tim Adams, 'Zen and the art of Robert Pirsig' in *The Observer*, 19 November 2006. https://www.theguardian.com/theobserver/2006/nov/19/features.review87.

10. Schopenhauer, quoted, John Gross (ed.), *The Oxford Book of Aphorisms*, Oxford University Press, 1983, p.342.
11. David Cassidy, *Could It Be Forever — My Story*, Headline Publishing, ebook, 2007, p.2704.
12. W. Somerset Maugham, *Collected Short Stories — Volume 1*, Penguin, 1984, p.401.
13. Ibid., p.404.
14. Laura Archera Huxley, *You Are Not The Target*, Avon Books, 1963, p.42.
15. Richard Morgan, 'Special One: Remembering José Mourinho's first-ever Chelsea press conference', *Sky Sports*, 18 October 2018. https://www.skysports.com/football/news/15116/11522231/special-one-remembering-jose-mourinhos-first-ever-chelsea-press-conference.
16. *Seinfeld*, The Café, 6 November 1991. https://seinfeldscripts.com/TheCafe.html.
17. Torben Betts, *Muswell Hill*, Oberon Books, 2012, p.59.
18. Niccolò Machiavelli, *The Prince*, 1513, Dover publications, 1992, p.46; my emphasis.
19. *London Calling* by The Clash, *Songfacts*. https://www.songfacts.com/facts/the-clash/london-calling.
20. Lyrics from The Clash song, *London Calling*, A-Z Lyrics. https://www.azlyrics.com/lyrics/clash/londoncalling.html.
21. Mark Vallen, 'London Calling – Selling out the legacy of Punk', Art For A Change. http://www.art-for-a-change.com/News/clash.htm.
22. Lyrics from The Clash song, *(White Man) In Hammersmith Palais*, CBS Records, June 1978. https://www.azlyrics.com/lyrics/clash/whitemaninhammersmithpalais.html.
23. The Jaguar London Calling Sales Event, YouTube, 15 October 2011. https://www.youtube.com/watch?v=6lbTsyrqXJs.
24. Rob Walker, 'Brand new Jag — The Clash sell luxury goods' in *The Boston Globe*, 15 September 2002. https://web.

archive.org/web/20021004114045/http://www.boston.com/dailyglobe2/258/focus/Brand_new_Jag%2B.shtml.

25. 'John Lydon butter commercial,' YouTube, 2 October 2008. https://www.youtube.com/watch?v=7mSE-Iy_tFY.
26. Joan Bakewell, 'My affair with Harold Pinter...' in *Mail on Sunday*, 16 January 2016. http://www.dailymail.co.uk/news/article-3402510/My-affair-Harold-Pinter-tainted-Betrayal-new-book-broadcaster-recalls-trauma-seeing-secret-romance-turned-hit-play.html#ixzz4CaIQEVeP.
27. The Edge, quoted, Julie Burchill, 'Stars in their own eyes' in *The Guardian*, 24 November 2001. https://www.theguardian.com/lifeandstyle/2001/nov/24/weekend.julieburchill.
28. Ibid.
29. Linnaeus, quoted Rudolf Rocker, *Culture and Nationalism*, Michael E. Coughlan, 1978, p.303.
30. German intellectuals, quoted, ibid., p.219.
31. German intellectuals, quoted, ibid., p.220.

Chapter 2

Meditation — The Remedy

Have you noticed your reaction when you've just passed the point of no-return in orgasm, when you've taken your first spoonful of ice-cold yoghurt, when you've taken your first mouthful of honeydew melon, when you're listening to your exact favourite part of one of your all-time favourite songs that you haven't heard for ages (in my case, the guitar break, 1 minute 45 seconds into Tahiti 80's *Swimming Suit*), and someone asks: 'Did you lock the front door?' or 'What do you think of Ryan Gosling?' or 'Have you eaten all the melon again?'

You feel put upon, pickpocketed. You feel trapped, because you know it's lose-lose; whether you answer or not, the moment has been sabotaged. Why? Because at the exact point when you most wanted to focus your attention on your sensations, feelings, you were dragged kicking and slurping back to thinking. You were prevented from fully feeling the sensation, sound or taste. Instead, you're now thinking about possible responses, even if it's just whether to answer at all. It makes no difference, you're in your head now — the link with feeling has been broken.

The point is deeply significant. If we can't think and feel at the same time, if the need is to focus on feeling without the impediment of thought, then clearly that focus, that awareness, is something other than thought. It can exist without thought. We can feel without thought. Or rather, we can only feel fully *without* thought.

Descartes was therefore wrong when he said 'I think, therefore I am'. Far better to say: I am *aware* that I think, I am *aware* that I feel, therefore I am.

I am not thought, I am awareness. I observe thoughts, none of which are me. Thoughts proliferate like bacteria under the warming rays of my awareness, but I can choose to focus on feelings instead.

If this realisation doesn't feel like the greatest revolution in your life, the dawning of a completely different possibility for happiness … give it time.

It makes sense, then, that most of us are unaware – or rather, that we do not *feel* – that thoughts make us miserable, and that a head crammed with thoughts makes us very miserable indeed. Why? Because we can't *feel* the damaging impact of thoughts precisely because we can't think and feel at the same time. Thought impedes our awareness of the damage it's doing.

As we will see in Chapter 4, humans who think too much lose contact with feeling. They are always thinking about Ryan Gosling, as it were, or about whether they have locked the front door. They are constantly distracted from feeling.

How does a head-trapped human sound? In 2021, the Scottish band Teenage Fanclub released a song, *The Sun Won't Shine On Me,* which goes:

> I have lost any sense of belonging
> I am drifting like ice on the sea
> With a troubled mind, I am in decline
> And the sun won't shine on me.[1]

A clue to the problem lies in the reference to 'a troubled mind' – there is no possibility of the sun shining through a headful of thoughts with which we identify as 'me'.

But we *all* have heads full of immiserating thoughts. We all think we are the complaining, grouchy little voice in our heads. The understanding that we are *the awareness* of the little voice – that the little voice is not, in fact, 'me' but a clanking, toxic, thought-generating machine that we can coolly observe, and if necessary, ignore – points the way to a simple but very profound solution. For the truth is that when we shift our focus of attention from our thoughts to our body, this mind machine is interrupted, quietened, perhaps even silenced.

An interesting question arises: how does miserable, head-trapped me feel when I start to separate myself from my thoughts, when the stream of miserable mentation subsides?

Midnight Thought Storm

Consider a common experience at night: a raging torrent of thought is passing through our head at 3 a.m.: 'I had the rest of the melon! So shoot me!' ... 'Gosling? I don't *care* about Gosling!' ... 'I've ruined everything by getting upset....'.

Over and over again we replay the same monologue, the same thoughts, churning the same anxiety in our chests. Night-time is a dangerous time for the head-trapped. The thought stream is generating so much stress, we are so much in our heads, that there is no possibility of relaxing into sleep.

We try to stop the thinking, but trying digs us deeper into the insomniac mire — after all, it's the problem mind trying to cure the problem mind's habit of overthinking by adding more thoughts! Sleep retreats even further.

We take a deep breath, try to switch off our thought process and things seem to calm down for a while; there is a moment of relaxation. And then a familiar little gremlin slips between our rib cage: 'Yes, she cleans the kitchen surfaces, but who throws the rubbish?' and off we go again. Thought is in the saddle, riding us.

Consider the state of our extremities under this thought blitz. Our toes are frozen chipolatas dangling from the ends of feet refrigerated by mind tension. Our hands are rigid, aching bird claws cramped by the mental onslaught, hanging on (to nothing) for dear life. It's as if thought generates so much heat, requires so much energy, that the rest of the body is deprived of both.

We can't think and feel at the same time. So, what happens when we reverse this trend, pull our attention away from thought and try to feel, say, our feet? Thought will certainly have something to say about it: 'Has she *ever* thrown the rubbish?!' and control will again be wrested back by the head. So, we again focus on our feet, just trying to detect any sensations.

Thought will reassert itself again and again, but we can keep noticing that it has grabbed our attention and we can return to sensations in our feet. This, by the way, is what people grandly call 'meditation'. Eventually, we will be able to feel something – the toes feel clenched and cold – and as we direct attention to these uncomfortable feelings, our toes and feet start to defreeze. We observe the thaw – warmth spreads through each toe; they start to glow. They are relaxing and loosening.

What's happening? It's not that we've got a warming mind-laser. Because we can't think and feel at the same time, because we're feeling our toes, thinking has subsided. And because it has subsided, the body starts to relax.

Then we can turn to focus on feeling our clenched hands. As they warm, they unclench in an aching but pleasurable relaxation, and defreeze. This all feels so much better, and when a thought pops up by way of a rear-guard action, we just roll our eyes. The appeal is so much less now that we feel warm and human; we don't want to deliver ourselves to that frigid torture chamber of the mind again.

Feeling nicely relaxed, having disrupted the thought stream so many times, the complaining, fretful impetus may begin to lessen – the mind gets fed up with being interrupted. At this point, we may fall asleep. This, of course, is all made much more difficult if the mind is deeply worried about something; or if it's frightened of not sleeping because we've got an important day tomorrow.

'Face It. Feel It Fully'

The mind harms us through the body — through the fear, anger, craving or jealousy it generates in our chests — but our body is our great ally in finding a solution.

Consider anxiety: we're on a packed plane and we hit some turbulence. The mind starts up:

> This is it, we're going down! The wings are going to break off, even modern jets can't take this much flexing!

This generates a surge of second-generation, adrenalised thought:

> I'm freaking out; I'm having a panic attack. What a lunatic! That guy's still calmly reading his book. People are noticing, they think I'm insane. *I am!* I've got to get out of here!

This generates more fear, which generates more terrorising thoughts.

Again, we can shift awareness from our thoughts to our body. We can place attention on the actual symptoms of panic. We can feel with as much intensity as possible the surge of adrenaline in our chests, the thumping of the heart, the rise and fall of our adrenalised lungs.

Here, we are not merely facing but *diving into* the sensations that constitute 'panic'. As in the night-time example, this shift of awareness — again, repeatedly contested by the mind, of course — interrupts the terrorising thought stream, which interrupts the triggering of adrenaline, so that the heart and lungs calm down.

It is a wonderful thing to plunge attention into the powerful thumping of the heart, to feel the lungs responding to the supposed 'emergency', and to watch as this change of focus breaks the vicious thought-emotion circle.

As we will discuss, this also works beautifully for grief, misery and deep sadness. We spend our time well when we read and remember the following comment from Eckhart Tolle:

> There are many pseudo escapes — work, drink, drugs, anger, projection, suppression, and so on — but they don't free you from the [emotional] pain. Suffering does not diminish in intensity when you make it unconscious...
>
> So don't turn away from the pain. Face it. Feel it fully. Feel it — don't think about it! Express it if necessary, but don't create a script in your mind around it. Give all your attention to the feeling, not to the person, event, or situation that seems to have caused it...
>
> So give your complete attention to what you feel, and refrain from mentally labelling it. As you go into the feeling, be intensely alert. At first, it may seem like a dark and terrifying place, and when the urge to turn away from it comes, observe it but don't act on it. *Keep putting your attention on the pain, keep feeling the grief, the fear, the dread, the loneliness, whatever it is.*[2]

This is wonderful advice. The results take us far beyond merely relieving the pain of disturbing emotions; with practice, they can be transformed from suffering into bliss. All we need to do is take some of the attention we obsessively focus outside and turn within.

Internal Flowers — The Big Surprise

If we focus on fear, grief, anger, resentment, lust, jealousy or despair enough times, the revolution happens; the revolution that we had not suspected was possible. Thinking subsides time and again, and suddenly tiny gaps start to appear between thoughts. In other words, we are left with awareness very temporarily unclouded by thoughts.

On a cinema screen, the unbroken flow of images ordinarily makes it impossible for us to see the white screen on which the movie is appearing. The screen is always there, of course, but it is hidden. If there is a pause in the flow of images, the screen is immediately visible. The same is true with the screen of awareness on which thoughts appear. When thoughts stop, the existence and nature of that screen can suddenly be detected, felt.

So how does it feel to be aware but thoughtless, if only for a micro-second? This is the real surprise.

The answer is that we feel bliss and love. Deeply unhappy though we may be at any given time, this is the real nature of our being; this is who we are. The misery is just a superficial tale told by a whirling shell of idiot thoughts signifying nothing about who we really are.

This is the phenomenon all meditators, all mystics, have described; a claim universally pooh-poohed as obviously too good to be true by head-trapped, heart-blocked intellectuals (more on them in Chapter 4). This is what mystics mean when they say things like 'The kingdom of heaven lies within'.

When the innate loving bliss of being breaks through the cloud of thoughts, this infamously suffering, fraught, even hellish, everyday world is transformed into a heavenly realm. It is experienced as paradise.

What on earth are we to make of this?

Just sitting, doing nothing — and, heaven knows, we may have been as miserable as sin 45 minutes earlier — a moment of no-thought, and suddenly a spark of delight in our chest, an ecstasy like the first stage of orgasm in what the Japanese call our *hara* (lower belly), an ecstatic tingling between our shoulder blades, in our lower back, in our armpits, on the instep of our ankle, in a toe, in our hands. It intensifies and spreads and becomes exactly the feeling of being deeply in love but without the anguish and craving.

All anxiety and sadness have been digested, their energy alchemised into love and bliss. Where there was once an inky-black, stagnant pool of sadness, self-hatred and despair, now love and delight shimmer like a golden pool of well-being in our bodies. The mystic Kabir gave instructions:

> Near your breastbone there is an open flower.
> Drink the honey that is all around that flower.[3]

It is indeed found near the breastbone, and we really can sip the honey by focusing attention there. This phenomenon is real; it *is* there!

Everything that comes into awareness now is delightful: the barking of a dog outside, a child's laughter, birdsong, the ragged snarl of a motorbike, even the shouts of people arguing – all drop like pebbles into this pool, generating ripples of delight. As we move our eyes around our room, every book, every ornament, generates joy. Kabir again:

> Don't go outside your house to see flowers. My friend, don't bother with that excursion. Inside your body there are flowers. One flower has a thousand petals. That will do for a place to sit. Sitting there you will have a glimpse of beauty inside the body and out of it, before gardens and after gardens.[4]

This flower with a thousand petals is Enlightenment.

The mystic master of yoga, Patanjali, said:

> *Nirodh Parinam* is the transformation of the mind in which the mind becomes permeated by the condition of *Nirodh* [bliss], which intervenes momentarily between

> an impression [thought] that is disappearing and the impression that is taking its place.[5]

Patanjali observed that thoughts pass as distinct, fleeting impressions in the mind. One thought passes and is gone; a second thought then arises, passes through and is gone. Because thoughts are separate there is a tiny space between them. When, in meditation, we are focused on feelings in the heart area, we can feel the bliss as it shines through this gap in thinking.

Experiencing this even in a small way, even once, has radical implications for our willingness and ability to meditate; the bliss of the internal treasure is such that we begin to lose interest in the lesser lures of external pleasures. In turn, this means that, deprived of the motivating force of craving and ambition, thoughts start to subside. It becomes easier to find gaps between thought, easier to feel the love and bliss.

In *The Power of Now,* Tolle writes of the psychological crisis that brought him to the verge of suicide:

> I woke up in the early hours with a feeling of absolute dread. I had woken up with such a feeling many times before, but this time it was more intense than it had ever been. The silence of the night, the vague outlines of the furniture in the dark room, the distant noise of a passing train — everything felt so alien, so hostile, and so utterly meaningless that it created in me a deep loathing of the world.[6]

This is the agonising experience of an overthinking, head-trapped human unable to feel the inherent bliss of being. We've all felt it at varying levels of awfulness in our daily lives. It is the polar opposite from the world experienced by the mystics where everyday objects appear like beloved friends populating an infinite garden of earthly delight.

Tolle moved through his suffering to an overwhelming experience of bliss that transformed his life. He offered this comparison: 'that which you realise within you, the power, is the cream, and everything else that you could achieve in this world is the skimmed milk'.[7]

The 'Divine Melody'

The delight of this 'cream' is so strange because, ordinarily, what we call happiness is inextricably linked to suffering: we enjoy food to the extent that we're hungry; we enjoy a cool drink to the extent that we're hot and thirsty. Pleasure is experienced precisely as a *release* from suffering. The English philosopher, John Stuart Mill, famously clarified his terms:

> By happiness is intended pleasure and the absence of pain...[8]

But pleasure and pain are conjoined at birth; there is always a downside to pleasure.

The phenomenon being described here is different. Initially, it may arrive as a tiny spark of bliss. We feel an odd tingling, a tickling in our chest that we have never felt before when sitting doing nothing. Osho communicated the sense of bewilderment:

> Something strange is happening, says Kabir. Some bells are ringing, but nobody is ringing them. There is some music, some melody, but he can't see anybody creating it.[9]

The 'music', the delight, is indeed uncreated, uncaused – it is the very nature of being, of awareness. Inside every human being, Kabir's 'divine melody' is always playing – it is always there, without fail, in all of us.

But if it is always there, if it is such a wonderful experience, why are so few people aware of it?

Because the thought stream that blocks awareness is relentless and ceaseless, even at night (dreaming is thinking in pictures), and because it takes between 40–45 minutes for an agitated mind to calm down sufficiently for this experience to arise in people who have never experienced it before.

It is fine to calm the mind and body somewhat by doing 10 minutes of *Calm* or *Headspace* meditation, but this experience needs one hour a day, preferably in the morning before the mind has been set ablaze with thought. And we can keep watching on and off throughout the day, noticing our emotional pleasures and pains. We need to watch our feelings like this consistently, for weeks, months, years, or as long as it takes. It is subtle, delicate and is, to a greater or lesser extent, blocked by excessive consumption of stimulants like caffeine and alcohol, which shoot the thinking mind into orbit. Eventually, inevitably, however, the phenomenon will be experienced.

We can begin by watching our feelings when we notice a wave of anxiety or sadness; we can just sit, relax and feel the emotion for ten minutes or so, just as an experiment. We can then try watching for longer. We can schedule a time every day when we sit alone and watch whatever feelings we can find for ten minutes, then twenty. We don't have to start by watching for an hour — that may seem like a big ask at first.

The problem is that the mind is a runaway train of thoughts; it doesn't want to stop. We try to feel emotions in our chest, and both before and after that attempt, we are thinking. So, we try again to feel any emotions in our chest. The problem with getting upset when feeling is yet again obstructed by thinking is that when we lift the lid off the word 'upset' and look inside, we find a whole lot of thinking. In other words, being bothered by thinking just intensifies thinking.

It is better to accept that this is just how all minds are. We have all been trained to think relentlessly, obsessively, without end. So of course the river of thought will keep sweeping us away from feeling. On the other hand, when we do get upset, that irritation is itself a feeling that we can use as a focus — watching the pain of irritation can lead us back into feeling. The same is true when we inevitably feel bored, anxious, sad, and so on.

We observe a train of thought steaming through, notice that we're thinking about a particular issue, and return to feeling. We recognise we're the witness, and remain open, aware of sensations and feelings. Another runaway thought train grabs us, and we notice we're on board, heading nowhere. We spot it and return to feeling.

It doesn't matter how many times we get carried away by thought; one day a gap *will* emerge, and the bliss will shine through. We may be completely beaten up and defeated by thoughts, by sleepiness, by lusty fantasies, by nostalgic longing, over and over again — it doesn't matter. We may be slumped against the meditational ropes, punch drunk, convinced we are the worst meditator the world has ever seen, but it really is a case of a thousand defeats and one victory. We just need that one victory.

And once that has happened, once love and bliss have broken through, the mystical cat is out of the bag. We now *know* that something is there — that the books we've read (like this one!) were not making it up after all. Of course, we still hesitate — our rational mind makes up all kinds of stories, accusing us of inventing, hallucinating, feeling what we wanted to feel — but part of us *knows* it is there now. And we know if it happened once, it could happen again. Revisiting the experience immediately becomes a priority in our life.

As we drop thoughts time and again, gaps start to open between thoughts and bliss slips through. Our enjoyable task, then, is to gently focus on the bliss wherever we find it.

There are, then, essentially two parts to this meditation: to watch sensations and emotions in the body and not follow interrupting thoughts, and to then watch the tiny glimmers, tinglings of bliss that arise. It is exactly as if a spark causes a piece of charcoal to catch light and glow — focusing on the bliss, on the glow, supplies oxygen fanning the flames.

The Unsinkable Heart

At first when we finish meditating, any bliss we've experienced quickly vanishes as we interact with the world — a Twitter spat here, an insult there, some depressing news, and the subtle 'divine melody' is lost beneath the roar of mental noise that seems so crucial in the moment. This is dismaying, disappointing, annoying. Our minds, always sceptical of the value of meditation (of not chasing pleasure), may question the value of dedicating so much time to meditating when even a hard-earned positive result is so fragile and transient.

But if we keep watching our thoughts, sensations and feelings, more sparks will fly, more charcoals will glow. Then, when we leave meditation, we can be sitting on the sofa, or bus, and glance inwards, and notice that the bliss is still there tingling, sparkling. We find that directing occasional inward glances at the glowing charcoal while talking (or while writing a book!) keep it glowing, prevent it from being overwhelmed by thought. In fact, the glow deepens and spreads. Eventually, we are able to keep it glowing through all kinds of annoyances and disturbances during the day. It's even there when we wake up in the middle of the night, and the next morning at breakfast. Then it disappears again.

Ordinarily, when we feel love and affection for someone, a wrong word, a tiny misunderstanding can cause that affection to flash into anger and hate, at which point all feelings of love vanish. Strangely, with meditative bliss, even when experiencing irritation, the feeling of love can continue in the background as an uninterrupted, ecstatic undercurrent. We continue to feel love even in a moment of mental upset. The irate mind does not completely obscure the inherent bliss of being; the glow of the charcoal continues to be detectable and can cause us to chuckle in the face of our own irritation.

Ordinarily, in response to a negative, unhappy event — say, an insult — it can feel like our heart has literally 'sunk' into a miserable dark hole in our chest. Having 'lost it' in this way, we may feel powerless to drag our hearts up out of the hole, no matter how much we would like to 'save' the evening, weekend or marriage.

With the bliss of meditation, the miserable hole into which the heart might otherwise sink is occupied; it's overflowing with delight. When an emotional disturbance happens, we can clearly feel that the heart has *not* 'sunk' into unhappiness in the usual way. We remain strangely buoyant, ecstatic, overflowing with this strange, uncaused, unconditioned and unconditional love.

It is quite something to encounter exactly the kind of negative event that has had us nose-diving into despondency and sadness thousands of times in the past bouncing off our bliss like a bullet bouncing off a tank. It reminds me of the scene in *Pulp Fiction* where hitmen, Jules and Vincent, are shot at with a fusillade of bullets at point-blank range. Checking themselves for wounds, they are amazed to find they are completely unharmed.

Similarly, old wounds may simply vanish; bitter arguments and resentments that might have been gnawing away at our hearts for hours or days are suddenly drained of all significance. It is exactly the feeling of being healed of those wounds.

As discussed in the previous chapter, the Suffering Ego is actually keen to emphasise the severity of its problems in hopes of attracting attention. When the emotional pain fuelling this ego is transformed into delight, there is a sense of liberation. We can see and feel with great clarity just how trivial an argument was, just how readily available solutions were all along.

We might previously have recognised the trivial basis of an argument, but our emotional pain made it impossible for us to stop fighting. Somebody spilled coffee all over a favourite book we leant them, lost a much-loved DVD, griped at us for not cleaning the bath properly, harshly accused us of opening a new packet of nuts before the old one was finished (the old one *was* finished!) ... It all seemed important, if only as a painful symbol of indifference, of a lack of love.

Buddhist teacher, Harvey Aronson, gave a very astute example of how pain and fear are often the real roots of anger:

> Most of us habitually think this way: 'Jayne lost the book I lent her. She is irresponsible and awful'. It is a lot harder to acknowledge this feeling: 'I fear I don't matter in her eyes. I fear she doesn't care for me. I fear I'm not very worthwhile'.[10]

With bliss, we don't feel that we are unloved, that love is lacking in our lives, *because we are full of love*. The sense of these 'disasters' is completely transformed. They look trivial, harmless, even funny; they are no longer damning evidence that we are unloved and unlovable. Without the pain, we are not *always* British Prime Minister, Neville Chamberlain, needing to face-down, rather than appease, a perpetually rampaging Hitlerian tyrant sitting next to us on the sofa.

Osho said:

> One has just to be here now [in the present, rather than in the mind] and then tiny, tiny moments, precious moments, will start dropping on you like a shower, a fine rain ... For a moment you are in utter bliss.

> And the strange thing is: when bliss is, you are not. For that moment you are not, only bliss is, overwhelming bliss, for no reason at all. It has been all along; it is just that you were not alert.[11]

These are indeed tiny, precious moments of delight. It may be a grey Monday morning at breakfast, and suddenly in response to a comment we find ourselves chuckling spontaneously, authentically, without inhibition or fakery. We might ourselves be completely taken aback – we don't laugh like that on a Monday morning! It is completely out of character. It is such a light, uninhibited, delighted laugh –– it feels like we haven't laughed like that since we were children. It was a childlike laugh! We just don't laugh like that. Was that me?! And we're giving out kisses and hugs to our beloved that would normally be made difficult or impossible by an underlying, pervasive tension, irritability and resentment.

One surprising result of this experience is that we realise that we have never been – at least, for as long as we can remember – truly happy. We have had excitement, eager expectation – plenty of expectation! – but it's always been mixed with anxiety, worry, fear of things going wrong, and awareness of inevitable eventual suffering and loss.

Too Good to Be True?

This experience of meditative ecstasy, this 'divine melody' of inner delight, is traumatic for us mere mortals. Our whole world-view may be based on the conviction that life is full of suffering, that misery predominates, that our individual happiness is doomed to be ravaged by old age and sickness.

As discussed, many of us have learned to use our sadness and suffering to attract sympathy and attention. Where does our discovery of an infinite source, not just of well-being, but of ecstatic, loving delight leave our Suffering Ego? Where does it leave our Righteous Ego, not to mention our Successful Ego?

Ironically, paradoxically, counter-intuitively, the most common response to the experience of meditative delight is fear, bewilderment and resistance. It seems far too good to be true! This just isn't how life is!

The first few times we experience this phenomenon we suspect that we must be imagining it, making it up. Our ego must be playing tricks on us, puffing itself up by, as it were, dressing up in the garb of a Buddhist monk the same way a toddler shuffles around in her mother's high heels to feel grown up.

On the other hand, when has anyone ever been able to trick themselves into transforming grief and misery into love and bliss? And actually, if that were possible through some kind of act of imagination, that would be amazing in itself, would it not? That would actually be worth pursuing!

Only after many repeat experiences does it become clear that this definitely is not some form of self-hypnosis, that the phenomenon is happening again and again in clearly similar ways under similar conditions. When we're thinking too obsessively, frantically, it doesn't happen. When we're trying too hard to make it happen — focusing on the happy future prospect of meditative bliss rather than on the barren or painful reality of what we're actually feeling here and now — it doesn't happen. When we relax without expectations and gently focus, suddenly it's there again. It becomes simply undeniable that there really is a source of limitless love and delight inside us that can be accessed when thoughts get out of the way.

A further reaction is guilt — we know ourselves only too well. We have our good sides, for sure, but we know how irascible, self-regarding, biased, ambitious, even violent, we are capable of being. We are used to experiencing moments of excitement, happiness, peace and anticipation but it seems impossible that someone as flawed, annoying and imperfect as 'me' could experience soaring delight and love for literally everyone, even our enemies. In life, you don't get anything for nothing; so, when we get *everything*, genuine contentment, by sitting doing nothing, we assume something must be wrong. We don't deserve it, perhaps we will be required to pay some terrible price. Could it be that we have simply gone mad?!

It would be typical of our life to date — of the fate that has always awaited our ordinary hopes and dreams — if this bright hope *also* turned out to be an empty promise. As author Truman Capote said:

> More tears are shed over answered prayers than unanswered ones.[12]

But this answer is different – our many disasters were rooted in our minds, our egos. This bliss is rooted in our hearts, in our very being.

There is also a deep sense of insecurity, turmoil and bewilderment. We have dedicated our entire lives to achieving happiness through various kinds of intense activity, movement, planning, plotting, spending and convincing. What on earth does it mean when we infinitely exceed the results of these ultimately futile efforts just by sitting on a sofa watching our thoughts and feelings? Where does this leave our ambition? Where does it leave our career, hobbies, romantic partnerships, friendships?

For example, what does a political activist writing about media bias, wars, injustice and climate change do now? Just carry on? But his immense efforts over decades have been based on a particular understanding of human nature and happiness. He assumed that spreading honest facts, honest opinions — that is, honest *thoughts* — about state-corporate greed and violence would make the world a better place. But he has now learned that thought as such, no matter how virtuous, *is the great obstacle* blocking the internal love and bliss that have the power to dissolve the human ego, the ultimate cause of all our problems. The issue now — quite clearly, undeniably, as he himself has experienced — is to *transcend*, not improve, thought.

As this indicates, the experience of loving bliss is the beginning of the end of ego. The dubious pleasures of attention seeking are now so clearly worthless compared to the ecstasy of inner awareness that the previously fierce desire to pursue name, game and fame, which got us into all kinds of trouble anyway, slowly starts to lose energy.

Hector the Helicopter's Dream

Hector the helicopter was in bad shape. From the dark confines of his hanger, the young, short-range whirlybird would often gaze in admiration at the huge, four-engine airliners as they returned from all corners of the Earth to chat about their adventures. One day, feeling more than a little foolish, having himself flown precisely *nowhere,* Hector plucked up courage and taxied over to join them. Alas, as he approached, the great airliners took one look at him down long noses and told him, in no uncertain manner, to reverse thrust and buzz off!

Taxiing back alone to his hanger, rotors drooping, Hector wept tears of frustration, wishing only that one day — *one day!* — he would be a source of pride to the airport.

It is at this point in the story that Hector's author, Arthur W. Baldwin, describes how, in the depths of despair, Hector dozes off and has a wonderful dream:

> Hector went to sleep that night and dreamed he was flying fast and high over mountains that were made of sugar plum pudding, circled by wide rivers of lemonade.[13]

As a child, I had the sweetest tooth imaginable. I lived for Anglo Bubbly bubble gum, wine gums, milk gums, sherbet fountains, Turkish delight, Caramac, on and on. My passion for sugary sweets was off the chart.

What took this to a whole different level were the exotic Swedish sweets to which I had access for one precious month a year, during the summer holidays we spent in my mother's hometown of Ystad. There was the caramel liquorice, the salt liquorice, the red liquorice, the salty liquorice bubble gum, the jelly dummies, worms, fishes, coke bottles. Then there were the foam sugar cubes, mushrooms and bananas (with and without chocolate), the outrageous super sour and super salt drops (both, like meditation, with sweet centres). And there were the amazing ice creams, never before tasted, with the caramel chocolate on the outside and soft nougat inside and the green marzipan cakes with vanilla cream that was on a completely different level from English cream. Not to mention the flying saucer-shaped marzipan cakes and my Swedish grandmother's hot rhubarb pie with ice-cold vanilla sauce and her hazelnut biscuits, almond cakes and ice-cold blueberry juice pressed into big bottles in the cellar.

As a sweet-obsessed child, then, Hector's dream, and particularly the illustration that accompanied it, stole my heart. The picture showed an open-mouthed, blissed-out Hector whirling over rivers of sparkling lemonade flowing around mountains of custard-covered plum pudding. My imagination went wild: the very earth must be made of bubble gum! I imagined sitting by a river, drinking ice-cold lemonade, twisting off some bubble gum, and chewing away to my heart's content. This was my idea of heaven.

In the illustration, Hector's entire world is transformed into a vision of delight. It is a vision of ecstasy. It seemed wonderful but impossible, of course. Even as a small child, I knew the world isn't really like that. The real world is made up of rocks and hard knocks, with rare, hard-won moments of pleasure — a bubble gum here, an ice cream there — but with so much frustration along the way. That's why we talk of 'the cold light of day', 'too good to be true' and 'rose-coloured spectacles'. We don't talk of 'too bad to be true'.

As a young adult, especially at night, I trembled before the unshakeable conviction, the complete certainty, that 'the cold light of day' revealed a grim universe where you (maybe) have fun when you are young ... but then life gets harder and harder as you gradually lose your vitality, your strength, your happiness, your loved ones, and ultimately your life. Could it possibly be denied that our lives just become greyer, harder, less pleasurable, more miserable: youth followed by old age; summer followed by winter; morning followed by night? It was just the way things were.

And then I persisted in my tragicomic efforts at meditation — thinking, fantasising, snoozing, remembering, fantasising again, snoozing again, writing paragraphs, emails and tweets in my head, groping year after year in the meditational murk.

And then, I didn't just share Hector's dream; I lived it. First one moment, then another, then another. In fact, incredibly — who would have guessed? — it turns out that the 'harsh reality' is the dream, is itself the head-trapped fantasy. Reality truly can be experienced as a limitless river of cool, sparkling lemonade; as a mountain range of custard-covered delight.

It does sound too good to be true, but it is true, nonetheless.

1. Teenage Fanclub, *The Sun Won't Shine on Me,* PeMa (Europe), 2021. https://www.azlyrics.com/lyrics/teenagefanclub/thesunwontshineonme.html.
2. Eckhart Tolle, *The Power Of Now*, Hodder & Stoughton, 2001, p.185; my emphasis.
3. Kabir, cited, Osho, *The Revolution*, Rebel Publishing, 2000, p.180.

4. Kabir, cited, Robert Bly (trans.), *The Kabir Book: Forty-Four of the Ecstatic Poems of Kabir,* Boston: Beacon Press, 1977, p.47.
5. Patanjali, cited, Osho, *Yoga – The Alpha and the Omega, Volume 7,* Rajneesh Foundation, 1977, p.59.
6. Eckhart Tolle, *The Power of Now,* Hodder and Stoughton, 2005, p.1.
7. *Eckhart Tolle Now* website, December 2020. https://members.eckharttolle.com/.
8. John Stuart Mill, *Utilitarianism,* Fount Paperbacks, 1979, p.257.
9. Osho, *The Guest* 13. https://oshoworld.com/the-guest-13/.
10. Harvey B. Aronson, *Buddhist Practice On Western Ground,* Shambhala, 2004, p.122.
11. Osho, *Don't Just Do Something, Sit There,* 1977, p.29. https://www.oshorajneesh.com/download/osho-books/darshan_diaries/Don't_Just_Do_Something_Sit_There.pdf.
12. Capote, Wikipedia. https://en.wikipedia.org/wiki/Answered_Prayers.
13. Arthur W. Baldwin, *Hector The Helicopter*, Reed International Books, 1964, p.4.

Chapter 3

Transforming Suffering into Love and Bliss

Removing the Splinter

Genuine solutions seem oddly absent.

Aid agencies seem unable to end world hunger. The UN seems unable to end war. Politicians don't prevent carbon emissions from rising. Doctors don't flatten global peaks of obesity, diabetes and Alzheimer's. Psychologists don't reverse historically high levels of anxiety and depression. And billion-dollar companies selling mindfulness don't offer much more than twenty minutes of relative calm.

Nothing seems to work. And there is a reason for it, as described in this Tibetan Buddhist anecdote:

> A butcher was grinding bones when a splinter got into his eye. He went to a physician who, instead of removing the splinter, gave him medicine to relieve the pain. The splinter continued to cause trouble, necessitating numerous visits to the physician who charged for each consultation. Eventually the physician left town. The butcher's son managed to remove the splinter, which finally brought lasting relief. Likewise, kings take money from the people but do not do their work.[1]

When large amounts of money and power stand to be gained by repeatedly *treating* a problem, it will tend to be relieved rather than cured. Over the course of centuries, powerful institutions will tend to grow out of this lucrative relief of symptoms. Indeed, their longevity and power, their grandeur, will make it difficult for us to perceive that *they*, often, are the greatest obstacles standing between us and genuine cures.

'Peace on earth and goodwill to all men' sounds like something everyone can applaud. And everyone *does* applaud. But as someone once observed, nappy factories and cruise missile factories have one thing in common: if the product isn't used, the factories close.

Tolstoy described how all kinds of impenetrable symbols and esoteric rituals have evolved to create an impression of meaning and virtue where none exist:

> Moreover, being all linked together, they approve and justify one another's acts — emperors and kings those of the soldiers, functionaries, and clergymen... while the populace, and especially the town populace, seeing nothing comprehensible in what is done by all these men, unwittingly ascribe to them a special, almost a supernatural, significance.[2]

Once someone has identified with these incomprehensible institutions — 'my party', 'my army', 'my government', 'my church' — we will have the devil's own task in getting them to question their allegiances. They will protect even their hell because it's '*mine*'! As we have discussed, if it's 'mine', it's part of 'me' and I will defend it as I would my very body.

No surprise, then, that the greatest friends of humanity — people genuinely motivated, truly able to supply answers — are deemed 'controversial'. 'In the land of the blind, the one-eyed man is king'? Absolutely not. In the land of the blind, 'the one-eyed man' is found nailed to the cross beside the fully sighted man and woman.

This is why, although solutions do exist, they are difficult to encounter. We *can* find genuine solutions, but we will have to find them ourselves with the help of rare individuals motivated by something other than personal profit.

If I could save one comment from the many books I've read on meditation, it might well be this one from Osho:

> You will have to dig like one digs a well. Layers and layers of mud ... and for days together you don't see any sign of water. Many times you become tired, exhausted, desperate.
>
> Many times you are so frustrated you stop digging, you say, 'It seems useless, futile. It seems there is no water here!' Many times in your spiritual journey this will come. But if you go on digging, one day the first signs of water will show. The mud is no more dry, it is wet — that wetness is called love. When in your inner being you go on digging and the mud becomes wet, you are getting love. Love starts flowing.
>
> It is muddy in the beginning, it is full of many other things. But one goes on digging ... the mud becomes less and less and more water will be flowing. One goes on digging ... then the mud disappears and fresh water will be flowing. One goes on digging ... and one has come to the source, to the springs. Now you can take as much water as you want and your well will never be empty. You can go on sharing, and the more you share the more you will be getting ... So go on digging so that you can have more. The more you have, the more springs will be pouring water in you.[3]

Watching the feelings, noticing thoughts and then returning to feelings sounds simple enough. And it is, but the reality is we will have to dig through layer upon layer of thought-mud.

For the first time in our lives we are fully feeling the emotional impact of the nostalgic daydreaming, the boisterous sexual fantasising, the bitter recriminations, the angry blaming, the passionate hoping, the searing guilt, and so on. We remember a painful loss and focus on the pain. We experience painful anxiety and focus on the fear. And not just once or twice; we have to dig through this mud over and over again. We notice the thoughts and return to feeling.

It is, at first, an extraordinary, absurd, utterly shambolic exercise. It's best not taken too seriously, because it starts out as a kind of disaster-comedy and continues that way for a long time. The idea that we can ape the Buddha's lotus position, fix a beatific smile on our face, and everything will be cool and dignified, is nonsense. It is much closer to think of our initial efforts as a kind of spiritual slapstick. Above all, we must not imagine that we have become 'holy' just because we have started watching our sensations, thoughts and feelings – that is the ego talking.

We have to dig through the mud of sleepiness, snoozing, nodding off, full-on actual dreaming, suddenly jerking awake and then remembering we're trying to notice our thoughts and watch our feelings.

As we relax more, we find ourselves digging through the mud of sexual fantasies, on and on – you've got to admire the inventiveness! Old loves are remembered, near-misses bitterly regretted, history rewritten, current possibilities plotted and planned. Don't take any of this too seriously. As the coolly understated line in Kurosawa's classic film, *The Seven Samurai*, observes:

> They say the fish that gets away looks bigger than it really is.[4]

That's fine – that's the mud, that's digging.

Then we dig into deeper, darker mud – the times we were embarrassed, humiliated, threatened, punched in the face for no reason, and no doubt very much worse – and we think of what happened, and what should have happened, what we should have done. It's like H. G. Wells' *The Time Machine* — our meditation seat races through time. We're supposed to be meditating, but our hands are clenched as we rewrite an old conflict in our heads from when we were a tiny tot. Fighting with a friend, aged 10, we rewrite what should have happened, shamelessly stealing a line delivered by John Wayne to Dean Martin in *Rio Bravo*:

> That's the second time you hit me. Don't ever do it again![5]

We release our imaginary foe, look around in surprise — 'Oh, it's decades later, I'm meditating and supposed to be watching my feelings'. That's fine; that's mud, that's us digging. The thing is to be as aware as possible when we're thinking and return to sensations and feeling. 'Failure' isn't failure; it's digging. Unawareness, forgetting *is* the mud. There's all manner of mud there — what do we expect?

It's not as grim as it sounds; there's a lot going on, quite a lot of it scandalous. If we approach our digging with an attitude of relaxed, even amused patience — not getting irritated, just accepting that the babbling mind is made up of layers and layers of thought-mud — we will quite soon notice something strange: tiny signs of faint moisture, a very weak glow of delight that we assume is our imagination, wishful-thinking.

And then, yes, we dig and dig and dig. We forget and then remember to watch, forget and remember — and, one day, the mud is genuinely wet! There it is! *We feel love!* It is beautiful. We're just sitting on the sofa bed alone in a room as usual and, after all that madness, after that great storm of thinking, fantasising and sleeping, *there is love in our heart!*

We assumed that digging was failing, that we were failing all along. Despite what everyone told us, we secretly believed that lots of digging without observable result was what happened when people were congenitally hopeless at meditating. We believed that meditating was not having any thoughts and feeling bliss. We thought digging was meditation-for-idiots, losers, people who had just accumulated too much mental crap to make any progress — no-hopers like us! To be honest, we secretly thought we were broken, intrinsically flawed humans, a 'wrong 'un'. So we never thought all this stuff would lead anywhere.

And, probably, we suspected that everyone talking of inner bliss was just involved in some kind of elaborate fraud — everybody's selling something, everyone has an angle. We thought we were just digging, round and round, in our own dirt. We're not spiritual beings, Buddhas — who did we think we were fooling?

And then ... Well, it seems we *were* digging in a meaningful direction after all. The 'wetness', the feeling of love, the speck of gold dust, quickly vanishes; but we know it's there now. We have an incentive to keep trying.

Then, and this truly is a big moment, the dawning of something momentous, the wetness of love appears *again*. We *didn't* imagine it before, because here it is again and it is *clearly exactly the same phenomenon*: the same love, the same bliss — there it is again! This is a very sobering moment. Subtle as it may be, this is arguably the most important moment in our lives thus far.

The feeling quickly disappears again, stubbornly refuses to return for days, weeks, even months, if we're trying too hard to feel it again — and then more wetness.

Now it is not just a distant gleam of love; a fresh stream of love is flowing through our hearts, cleansing us. It is a very definite, powerful presence. There is no room for doubt now — it's there. It's real. Our life has changed. Everything else is nonsense. We know that this is the only real delight and happiness worth bothering about. It seems wrong to call it 'happiness', because all experiences associated with that word are tainted with unhappiness in a way that this is clearly not. As discussed in the last chapter, worldly 'happiness' comes with anxiety, is painful with excitement; it's tiring, even exhausting. It reaches a peak and then falls and we will likely feel down, drained afterwards. We crash from a peak experience to the valley floor, like World Cup winner, Geoff Hurst (see Chapter 4).

The flowing of Osho's 'fresh water' is different. It's cooling, not exciting; it's soothing, ecstatic, blissful. It's refreshing, not exhausting. It is not followed by a down. But what is really revolutionary is that the bliss is accompanied by love.

Ordinary happiness can be cold, anxious, tetchily self-regarding. We may become furious when people threaten to obstruct or spoil our happiness in any way. But this bliss is accompanied by a warm feeling of love for others. The urge is to say warm, kind things; to give money, gifts, help, whatever; to hug and kiss and hold.

This is decisive because we can imagine somehow hypnotising ourselves to feel blissfully happy, if only to reassure ourselves that we're not complete idiots sitting there on that time-travelling sofa bed, or wherever we sit, hour after hour. But we *cannot* believe that we are also able to invent this feeling of love. Why? Because it's beyond anything we've felt before. We've never felt intense love for nobody in particular when just sitting doing nothing — it's not possible! And we've certainly never felt love for a complete stranger, or somebody we can't stand.

Only very occasionally have we come close to the feeling in romantic relationships and with close family when there has been some deep personal investment. We showered love on our romantic partner, or on our grandmother, because they were important to us. But now, for example, we're feeling love for a person who happened to come to mind who has been pursuing us for years in a campaign of vengeance, who hates our guts.

That's insane, completely beyond our normal way of being. We're not capable of making that up. Why would we? We're thinking of his name and his effortlessly punchable face, and in place of the usual hostility, the fresh water of love flows freely on. How utterly bizarre! When we leave the sofa bed, the water continues flowing and we feel love for everyone we see.

But even now we should not get carried away because, believe it or not, mystics urge us not to settle for mere trifles like the eradication of emotional suffering. They seriously urge us to understand that happiness is not a big deal – it's quite easily achieved; it's just the start of a journey into much deeper delight.

The 'fresh water' of loving bliss will continue to flow more and more strongly, revealing previously unimagined mysteries and wonders. We are told that enlightenment itself goes on deepening, revealing more and more treasures, without end.

Ballad of the 'Broken-Hearted' Ego

A Sufi tale has it that God plays a joke on us when we're born. He whispers in our ear:

You are the special one!

The joke is that he says it to *everyone* – you, me, José Mourinho, everybody.

As discussed in Chapter 1, we are born without any idea of who we are. Clues are reflected back at us by the spinning circle of mirrors. Ego itself is an empty whirlpool of impressions made up of these reflections – beautiful in a way, but shockingly insubstantial.

On arriving here, 'Who am I?' With her beaming smile and adoring blue eyes, my mother holds me up and tells me: 'You're like marzipan; I could eat you all up'. My father tells me:

'You've got big hands, perfect for playing the piano'. Later, his threatening scowl tells me I've been 'bad', 'selfish'.

Inevitably, the opinions of others are very important to me — my self-esteem, my confidence are all tied up with their reactions. With a few words, a complete stranger who knows nothing about me can inflict serious damage on my ego. Consider all of this in relation to one common, life-altering scenario…

Somehow gathering courage he didn't think existed, a teenager at a party sidles up to the table filled with snacks and booze and makes a jokey aside to an attractive girl pouring herself a drink. To his amazement, because he knows she is way out of his league, she laughs and smiles at him with real delight, as if she had been *hoping* he would talk to her.

She, in turn, is amazed that his face has lit up with exactly comparable enthusiasm; she hadn't imagined he'd be remotely interested in talking *to her*. They continue joking and laughing as if they've known each other for ages. It's almost embarrassing how obviously enthusiastic they both are — people will notice!

In short, they both find each other attractive, interesting, funny, and are tremendously flattered that such a 'catch' is giving them this level of massively positive attention. It's an incredibly encouraging reflection to add to the many other reflections they've received over the years. This is great news! Wonderful! They feel like they're floating on cloud nine.

Indeed, this reflection, blazing bright, overwhelms all the fading, older reflections and rejections that don't matter anymore, because that's all in the past now — the times when they were cold-shouldered, treated with agonising indifference, even contempt. They feel renewed, healed, as those old wounds and doubts are swamped by this new affirmation: 'A wonderful person thinks I'm wonderful!' They could, and do, weep tears of joy.

Unsurprisingly, we view the person reflecting this opinion of us as our true friend. Really, no-one else treats us this way; so we hold onto them tightly, value them, treasure them for supporting such a beautiful self-image. We say: 'I love you, I love you. I will *always* love you. I would do anything for you'.

Then, one impossible day, they are in a club and his (to be fair) charming friend asks her to go downstairs for a dance. To his abject, paralysing horror, the twinkle in his friend's eye finds a match in her own, and she's gone. Not exactly in that moment, not that dramatically; but anyway, she's gone.

It's over and what does it mean? It's clear that she finds his friend even more interesting, gorgeous, amusing and wonderful. The wondrously positive reflection has simply vanished.

These are traumas we never forget. We consider them our great, formative heartbreaks. It feels for all the world like love. But what got broken: our heart, or our ego?

'I Like You, but I Don't Love You...'

When she finished with him, she killed him as part of her life. He disappeared from her world; she from his. He loved her – she had been at the centre of his thoughts each day, every day, for weeks, months, maybe years – but now he's not part of her life at all. It's as if they both died to each other. Evicted from the nucleus, he is not even part of her circle of friends, nor even the outer shell of orbiting colleagues and casual acquaintances. Standing alone in a queue it occurs to him that he's further removed from her now than the guy who serves her at the local supermarket.

It hurt him when she said, 'I don't love you', but it broke his heart when she said:

> Please, accept this situation, because it's hard for me to have you suffering in this way.

To be so obviously an object of pity, rather than of love — and he can feel now, viscerally, just how poles-apart love and pity are — denied him even the solace and dignity of hope. Intentionally or not, her expression of pity felt savage, brutal. It was the sound of a door being slammed on love — 'mercifully', 'compassionately' — forever. His ego rages:

> Who said anything about me 'suffering'? Who says I've been suffering *that* much? What makes you so high and mighty? I was keen, but I wasn't grovelling in the dirt.
>
> 'Please', I have to 'accept this situation'? Do I?! What, is she worried that I *won't* accept it and become a stalker?! Is her concern to assuage her guilt, to protect *herself* from suffering? How could it be more brutal, more demeaning?

If he thinks she is hurting at the thought of his hurt, a clear temptation will be to seek to punish her with *his* suffering. The Suffering Ego looms large. He will make it clear just how much pain she has caused him, just how 'cruel' and 'unfair' she has been. His ego has been humiliated and it wants to 'balance the books'.

The Suffering Ego believes that, if it suffers enough, some positive outcome will result — attention, sympathy, support. He develops a motivation to intensify his suffering as far as possible, to wallow in it, maximise it. Maybe the cosmos will detect his misery and intervene to help him. Maybe *she'll* save him. More likely, her feelings of pity will grow, intensifying the whole sense of humiliating imbalance. He may come to perceive every kindly word as a patronising, self-serving attack. Where will that leave him then: obsessed but unable even to talk to her? My god, is he going to actually *become* a stalker? Is that who he is? Was she right about him after all?

And then he finds out she's seeing someone else. Or that she's seeing his friend, perhaps even his best friend.

At this point, the pain in his chest lights up like one of those giant Hollywood searchlights. Except this one's designed by H. R. Giger and is not delivering white light but inky-black thoughts cascading through his head. Now, thoughts like the memory of her saying, 'It's hard for me to have you suffering in this way', become truly agonising as they pass through his mind and body.

The agony can seem almost unbearable; he literally winces, cries tears of pure pain. This agony fuels more poison jetting from the black searchlights, more thoughts drenched with suffering.

As we know only too well from our newspapers, this vicious circle of pain can spiral down into literally any extreme of obsession, madness and hatred; even suicide and murder. Months and years can be spent gnawing at the wound, adding fuel to a Suffering Ego that makes ever more desperate, futile attempts to end the pain.

Jumping into the Tiger's Mouth

But, as we also now know, there *is* a way to transcend this misery. It is worth quoting Eckhart Tolle again:

> There are many pseudo escapes — work, drink, drugs, anger, projection, suppression, and so on — but they don't free you from the pain. Suffering does not diminish in intensity when you make it unconscious...
>
> So don't turn away from the pain. Face it. Feel it fully. Feel it — don't think about it! Express it if necessary, but don't create a script in your mind around it. Give all your attention to the feeling, not to the person, event, or situation that seems to have caused it...

> So give your complete attention to what you feel, and refrain from mentally labelling it. As you go into the feeling, be intensely alert. At first, it may seem like a dark and terrifying place, and when the urge to turn away from it comes, observe it but don't act on it. Keep putting your attention on the pain, keep feeling the grief, the fear, the dread, the loneliness, whatever it is.[6]

This is a new approach and it takes us very, very far away. Forget for the moment about 'solving' the problem through doing, acting, speaking — *I'll show her! I'll make him see!* — just face the pain, feel it fully. Feel it! As spiritual teacher Michael Singer wrote:

> If you want to be free, you must first accept that there is pain in your heart. You have stored it there. And you've done everything you can think of to keep it there, deep inside, so that you never have to feel it. There is also tremendous joy, beauty, love, and peace within you. But they are on the other side of the pain. On the other side of the pain is ecstasy. On the other side is freedom. Your true greatness hides on the other side of that layer of pain. You must be willing to accept pain in order to pass through to the other side. Just accept that it is in there and that you are going to feel it. Accept that if you relax, it will have its moment before your awareness, and then it will pass. It always does.[7]

There are many creative strategies for escaping from a man-eating tiger about to sink its teeth into you; by far the most interesting and elegant is to stop, turn and jump into the tiger's mouth.

In Buddhist iconography, the tiger's mouth of worldly suffering is represented by the fierce Guardians that stand outside temple entrances. Beyond, inside the 'mouth', the temple — a place symbolic of unimagined wonders — stands a gleaming golden statue of the Buddha, a hand extended in welcome and reassurance; a loving, blissful smile on his face. The statue, the Buddha, is a symbol of our own loving bliss — it's us. This is our real identity, who we are.

How do we jump into the tiger's mouth, how do we enter the temple? By entering deeply into the pain represented by the temple guardians.

He loved her, he adored her, and she preferred someone else. The pain is real, terrible, but it can become the portal to an experience of loving bliss that is almost impossible to describe. The American mystic, Robert Adams, tried his best:

> I felt a love, a compassion, a humility, all at the same time. That was truly indescribable. It wasn't a love that you're aware of. Think of something that you really love, or someone that you really love with all your heart. Multiply this by a jillion million trillion, and you'll understand what I'm talking about.[8]

Beyond the guardians, the teeth, the pain, the gleaming, golden reality of loving bliss is waiting.

The mind is hopeless at managing pain. We can *do*, and act, and manipulate, and change the world in any number of ways, but the emotional pain will remain. The pain is a feeling, not a thought, and it needs to be digested through meditation, witnessing.

We have to dig through the mud. No matter how terrible the pain, a meditator can see that the latest heartbreak has really done nothing more than dump a few more layers of obscuring mud over the heart. We can face this new pain-mud, too — we can watch it, feel it, dig through it.

However agonising the loss — the grief, the dreadful injustice — we know that, if we can keep digging, we will arrive at the 'freshly flowing water', the release of loving bliss. It is always there, and it holds out an invincible promise of an ecstasy and love beyond anything experienced in any love affair, in any standing ovation, in any bloated bank balance.

Everything we could have dreamed of — and far, far more — is waiting for us. We know that, if we keep digging, even this pain we are experiencing can be left far behind.

The Art of Do-It-Yourself Ultimate Romance

Is romantic love just the play of egos, then? Is there nothing more to it than that?

Well, when we do genuinely fall in love, the intensity of our concern for the other can be such that we forget ourselves altogether. The strength of our love, of feeling, can mean that we lose interest in the usual egotistical ambitions driving our frenzied mental activity. As though bewitched by love, our minds fall silent. There's nothing more to want, nothing more to need — he or she is everything to us — so mental activity subsides.

In these moments of natural meditation, loving bliss does indeed blaze from our hearts. When two people feel this way at the same time, it is a heavenly experience of genuine love rather than mutual ego-reinforcement. How to tell the difference? Desire is serious, dark, sad, heavy, painful, full of gravity, all about getting. Love is joyful, bright, weightless, full of light, all about giving. Desire feels like it has never got enough. Love feels like it has never given enough.

Feeling this way with a particular person, we mistakenly assume that he or she is the *cause* of the bliss. In fact, the bliss is uncaused; it arises from our stumbling into a meditative state. This is why the experience of loving bliss in meditation is exactly that of falling in love (minus the anguish).

Having made this mistake, we naturally tend to centre our lives around this blissful, magical being. Alas, the great calamity of young love is that we are often not yet centred in ourselves and instead seek, and think we have found, our centre in some perfect partner — 'The One'. The more we look for happiness outside ourselves in this way, the more we move away from the real source of happiness within. All kinds of trouble must ensue.

And when we lose 'The One', the disaster seems near-absolute. We feel as though we've lost a blue-moon possibility of happiness — it's never happened before and we suspect it will never happen again.

But the chances are actually very high of meeting 'The One', if we become centred in ourselves; if we sit in meditation watching our sensations, thoughts and feelings.

After meditating, we can meet 'The One' raising a short, scruffy leg against a lamppost. We can meet 'The One' posting a letter through our letterbox, or handing us our receipt in the supermarket. We can meet 'The One' struggling with his or her walking frame.

When we learn the art of do-it-yourself ultimate romance by uncovering the loving bliss hidden beneath that bad old cloud of ego-driven thought-drivel, it feels as though *everyone* is 'The One'. Then, the loss of particular relationships is tremendously sad, of course, but not the utter tragedy we previously imagined.

Imprisoned in Bliss

Eva cleans toilets for a living. She works for some vast, trans-European cleaning conglomerate with an ugly, jagged acronym for a name. They give her the same shapeless blue uniform and black plastic clogs they give all their cleaners. She has to wear them. They make her look like some kind of inmate. At the end of every shift, she has to text the company from her mobile, so GPS can verify she is where she's supposed to be.

Until very recently, Eva has been one of the most vibrant, enlivening people I've ever met. She's always got time for a quick chat; always got some outrageous anecdote to relate. For years, she's loved working among the trees and flowers of the park. She doesn't mind the work and her toilets are always sparkling, spotless. She often says things like:

> Everyday, I feel thankful that I can work in such a beautiful place.

She's well aware that the company doesn't give much of a damn about her. To them, she's one more low-paid worker doing a low-skilled job. If she performs to the required standard, fine. If she doesn't, she can be replaced by somebody who does. They wouldn't notice the change, wouldn't blink an eye. It doesn't matter to them that she does a fantastic job with real joy, each time, every time.

Recently, as part of a revenue drive, the company that owns the buildings her company is responsible for cleaning has started hosting music concerts in the park, as well as parties, even weddings (sometimes several per day). Eva has to clean up the additional mess in the toilets, in the grounds, on her own, for the same pay. Sometimes she has to work extra time to clear up the vomit and broken glass.

As noted, she is normally a ray of light. But now she feels exploited — the 'company', the 'system' is taking advantage of her. She knows there's no escape for low-paid, low-skilled workers — any other company will be more or less the same. She feels trapped, angry, tiny, helpless. She is full of sadness, resentment, bitterness and pain.

Everything she says about 'the system' is true; the world really is this way, particularly for low-paid workers. One can argue that the blame belongs to 'them', but the suffering certainly belongs to her.

Unfortunately, when the blame belongs to 'them', the solution also belongs to 'them' — 'they' have to do something, 'they' have to change; only that can alleviate her misery. But in dealing with that pain, she can't wait for the company, the global economic system, the world, to change. That's not going to happen any time soon. It may never happen.

One way of dealing with the pain is for Eva to take solace in a Suffering Ego. She can gain the satisfaction of feeling a victim, of winning sympathetic attention by repeatedly describing the facts of the injustice and hopelessness of her situation to anyone willing to listen.

In this case, she may find herself in a vicious circle. She may start to gain ego satisfaction, a certain reward, from her problems. She may become focused on complaining rather than on doing anything about the situation. She may angrily dismiss suggested solutions out of hand — that she could talk to management, join a union, find another job.

Alternatively, without for one moment resigning herself to the injustice of her situation, without simply accepting her lot, she could use the pain as a portal, as a way to dissolve the Suffering Ego and all other forms of ego.

If this sounds like insultingly apolitical, happy-clappy, navel-gazing that will never help Eva in any way at all, consider the remarkable story of Ananta Kranti.

In his book, *Extraordinary Awakenings*, psychologist and meditation teacher, Steve Taylor, tells of how Ananta had been a sannyasin in Osho's commune in India where she learned to watch thoughts and feelings in meditation. While subsequently working in Japan, she unwittingly got caught up in a drugs bust and spent three years in prison in appalling conditions. Forbidden from speaking, the prisoners — convicted murderers among them — worked long shifts in a factory as virtual slave labourers. As the only Westerner in her block, Ananta was a particular target for aggression.

Experiencing deep psychological and physical suffering, she came to a point where the misery of her existence was simply overwhelming:

> All I had in my cell was some Osho books that a friend had given me during my trial. I would read a couple of pages after coming back from the factory, and the wisdom would go deep inside me, directly and immediately.
>
> One day I came back to the cell from the factory and was just about to start reading but couldn't. I was in too much pain. I lay back and dropped into the pain ... I lay back and kept dropping and dropping into the pain. It was excruciating, but I had to surrender to it. There was nothing else left to do.
>
> Then I dropped into a space where the physical body was no more. Whatever I dropped into just kept opening and opening, into more and more light, beauty, gratitude, freedom ... I just kept letting go and dropping and dropping. There was only this — this beautiful love and bliss.[9]

Ananta said that, thereafter, she constantly had 'an inner smile':

> I was in a constant state of bliss, even though the same conditions and difficulties continued in prison.[10]

Eva can follow the same path as Ananta. Yes, she is suffering from injustice, exploitation, callous corporate indifference — all this is true. But she can drop into her pain; she can keep dropping and dropping into her pain. Eventually, a moment will come when that pain opens into 'light, beauty, gratitude, freedom', a 'beautiful love and bliss'. If it can happen in a brutal, violent prison environment, it can happen on the sofa in the lounge before and after work. This is real-world meditation. It is a real answer to the immediate problem, alchemising psychological and emotional pain into delight.

Forget properly remunerated toilet cleaning, it results in an attainment that exceeds anything provided by even the most exalted job with the most astronomical pay, with the greatest status and rewards. This is the profound, life-changing discovery of treasure hidden in the human heart. Once attained, all forms of suffering and dissatisfaction can be digested, alchemised in the same way.

On a practical level, love and bliss dissolve the Righteous and Suffering Egos. We no longer have any investment in the pain, in advertising our pain. We now obviously have all the incentive in the world to digest and alchemise the pain, to be free of it, rather than clinging to it as a way to feel 'special', 'especially' exploited.

And then the irony — the result of this much-derided 'navel-gazing', this inactivist pause in our compulsive activism — is that positive pragmatic actions and solutions become much more possible.

Digesting and alchemising the pain does not mean we simply accept further injustice, the imposition of further pain. It means we're freed from pain and ego to respond positively; to talk, take action, to leave, and so on. And to take action out of love and bliss, rather than misery, is an extraordinary thing. It is a rare phenomenon, not normally seen. It has a way of working wonders. The writer, Bill Moyers, asked comparative mythologist, Joseph Campbell:

> Do you ever have this sense when you are following your bliss, as I have at moments, of being helped by hidden hands?[11]

Campbell replied:

All the time. It is miraculous. I even have a superstition that has grown on me as the result of invisible hands coming all the time — namely, that if you do follow your bliss you put yourself on a kind of track that has been there all the while, waiting for you, and the life that you ought to be living is the one you are living. When you can see that, you begin to meet people who are in the field of your bliss, and they open the doors to you. I say, follow your bliss and don't be afraid, and doors will open where you didn't know they were going to be.

Desire: 'Something to Yield To or Be Overcome?'

Halfway through the first concert of rock band The The's 'Comeback Special' tour at the Royal Albert Hall in June 2018, singer-songwriter Matt Johnson took to the stage alone with his acoustic guitar and sang *True Happiness This Way Lies*, from the album *Dusk*. He sang about a key issue at the heart of human desire:

> And have you ever wanted something so badly
> That it possessed your body and your soul
> Through the night and through the day...
> Until you finally get it...
> And then you realise *that it wasn't what you wanted after all?*[12]

The problem is not just that we can't get what we want. The problem is that we often *can*, but when we do, we *still* 'can't get no satisfaction'. What then?

> And then those self-same sickly little thoughts
> Now go and attach themselves to something ... or somebody ... new.

> And the whole ... goddamn ... thing ... starts ... all over ... *again!*

This, by the way, is exactly what Buddhists mean by *samsara*: the mind feels desire; it gets; it loses interest in what it gets and desires something new. With the whole process endlessly rotating like a wheel. It is crucial to understand that the mind is not interested in what it has; it is only interested in what it lacks. By definition, then, the mind cannot find satisfaction — it must always be yearning, moving.

With rare honesty, on classic albums like *Infected, Mind Bomb* and *Dusk*, Johnson explored this question facing us all — what are we to do about relentless, nagging desire? More specifically, what are we to do about sexual desire?

The difficulty being, as Johnson reminds us, that indulgence does not cool but inflames desire, pours petrol on the fire. Indulgence promises but does not deliver contentment. Instead, it generates addiction that torments us with the law of diminishing returns. The more we get, the more we want, because the more we get, the less we enjoy what we get. This can start to eat away at our integrity, our sense of who we are:

> I was trying so hard to cleanse myself
> I was turning into somebody else.
> I was trying so hard to *please* myself
> I was turning into somebody else.[13]

Alas, no matter how maddening the torment of insatiable indulgence, the alternative — repression, self-denial — seems merely to put a cork in volcanic cravings which will subsequently erupt with ever greater intensity. Religious organisations the world over bear witness to the catastrophic failure to impose chastity through force of will. The volcano remains active – the energy will out, no matter how destructively.

With sex addicts to the left of us, paedophile priests to the right, we're stuck in the middle with The The asking of lust:

> Is it something to yield to or be overcome?[14]

Neither of these seem to offer much hope.

Back at the Royal Albert Hall, Johnson continued with his solo acoustic number on the same theme:

> Well, I've been crushing the symptoms
> But I can't locate the cause.
> Could God *really* be so cruel,
> To give us feelings that could never be fulfilled?
> *Baby!* ... I've got my sights set on you.
> I've got my sights set on you.
> And someday, someday, someday ... you'll come my way.
> But when you put your arms around me,
> I'll be lookin' over your shoulder for somethin' new.
> Cause I ain't ever found peace upon the breast of a girl...

Remarkably, at this point, Johnson stopped singing and started critiquing his own song to the audience:

> I always have to add a disclaimer there ... Because I've found a lot of peace on the breast of girls. Haven't we all? From infancy, all the way to old age, there's no place like home, and there's no home like the breast of a girl.

It was a brilliant, hilarious comment, but it suggested moments of reprieve rather than a genuine answer to the problem. Johnson then resumed his song:

> Cause I ain't ever found peace upon the breast of a girl.
> I ain't ever found peace with the religion of the world.
> I ain't ever found peace at the bottom of a glass.
> Sometimes it seems the more I ask for, the less I receive.
> Sometimes it seems the more I ask for, the less I receive.
> The only true freedom is freedom from the heart's desires
> And the only true happiness this way lies.

Yes, we all sense it lies in that direction — we've heard any amount of spiritual gossip from enlightened mystics to that effect. But how, actually, are we to be free of the heart's insatiable desires? Is our only hope to wait for the cell door to creak open of its own accord as we sink into sexual decrepitude? And, frankly, even if we lose functional capacity, will we ever *really* lose that relentless twinkle in our eye?

Keeping Company with Desire

Bizarrely, given that he had long been one of my musical heroes, Johnson had actually interviewed me, in 2015, for his *Radio Cineola* project. The interview was focused on my political writing for *Media Lens*, but I couldn't resist taking the chance to ask him about lyrics that had been haunting me for 30 years. And so, after a civilised, head-based discussion about media bias — how important it is to master the tools of intellectual self-defence, all that stuff — I felt a little awkward going off-topic. I asked:

> So, what about desire, Matt? Did you ever find a solution to the problem of always wanting more, of indulgence making it worse?

Johnson laughed, hesitated and responded cautiously — understandable, but somewhat chucklesome given the very frank lyrics and artwork he has unleashed on the public:

> Well, it's always there, isn't it? ... waiting to pounce on you.

Again, it sounded like he had developed coping strategies rather than solutions. On the other hand, it was an awkward subject to discuss with a near-complete stranger.

So, what is the response of every one of the mystic masters of meditation over the last 10,000 years to the big question of big desire: 'Is it something to yield to or be overcome?'

Their answer, amazingly, without exception: Do nothing, just watch!

Indulgence is fine, if we're happy as we are, enjoying our sexuality; there's nothing wrong with it. It gives momentary pleasure — a high-energy peak experience inevitably followed by a low-energy trough experience. But, as discussed, indulgence does not relieve the thirst of desire. On the contrary, the habit is thereby deepened, entrenched.

Similarly, repression is like attempting to push water gushing from a fountain back to the source — the energy will erupt with even greater force. This is the disaster that has befallen so many attempts at repression. So where does that leave us? Zen Master Yagyu said:

> Let yourself go with the desire. Be with it, keep company with it. This is the way to get rid of it.[15]

The advice: just observe the sexual energy, feel it. Become deeply, intimately acquainted with the experience of sexual desire. At first sight, this may look like a futile strategy, but it is not.

Firstly, watching desire intensely — feeling that fiery energy in our bodies, watching the thoughts that cascade — annihilates many of the illusions that we have about desire. For example, we take it for granted that desire is an entirely positive thrill, a great entertainment. But careful observation reveals that the thrill is uncomfortable, wearing, stressful. Desire is nagging, bullying, even maddening. As Montaigne said so well:

> Pleasure chews and grinds us.[16]

When we watch desire often, closely, for a long time – when we just sit and let it sizzle and smoulder away in our bodies – we become more sensitive to what is really the case. There is a wonderful insight to be gained here. A Buddhist text comments:

> If you have an eyelash and put it on the palm of your hand, you cannot feel it. If that eyelash were put on the eye, though, it would cause pain and you cannot be at rest.[17]

Closely observing our feelings in meditation slowly increases our sensitivity. From being as sensitive to the painful reality of desire as the palm of a hand, we become as sensitive as the surface of an eye. And it is exactly this difference that separates a blindly enthusiastic sex addict from an enlightened mystic. The effort is not to create any particular feeling, it is to patiently observe whatever is there.

Three things happen when we observe desire closely. First, we feel the painful reality of desire more clearly and it loses some of its allure. Second, a distance is created between our witnessing consciousness and desire, which disrupts our habitual identification – we are not desire; we are *the witness* watching desire. Third, as discussed in previous chapters, that painful energy can be transformed into bliss.

Under observation the energy of lust can suddenly alchemise into loving bliss (*metta*). Because the former is thrilling but uncomfortable and the latter deeply blissful, peaceful, the exact moment of change can be felt very clearly. Lama Zopa Rinpoche commented:

> We can immediately feel the freedom. Our mind is no longer sharp and hurtful like a thorn bush or rough and hard like a rock, but smooth and blissful like cream. Our heart feels open and spacious, and we immediately experience peace and happiness.[18]

This recalls Eckhart Tolle's comment from Chapter 2: meditation, awareness allows us to experience 'the cream' while 'everything else that you could achieve in this world is the skimmed milk'.[19]

This is the ultimate answer to the question posed by The The: simply watching sexual energy will eventually alchemise painful lust into blissful love. Because this is very clearly, undeniably 'the cream', the issue of whether we should indulge or repress sexual desire falls away. No willpower is needed — we always thought sex was 'the cream', but now we realise it is the 'skimmed milk'. Nothing wrong with it in an occasional cup of tea, but this other thing is very obviously the way to go.

This is the alchemy that transforms base metal emotions into spiritual gold. It is the meaning behind the Buddhist symbol of the pristine, beautiful 'lotus' of spiritual ecstasy arising out of the 'mud' of the body and its desires.

The 'mud' is not 'disgusting' or 'shameful' — it is energy and life; it is the very basis of spiritual growth and *not* to be rejected. It is to be accepted, embraced, enjoyed and transformed into higher forms of energy and delight, as and when we are ready. All other desires and forms of addiction to external pleasures can be watched and transformed in exactly this way.

The astonishing, near-complete refusal of the cultural 'mainstream', and of the head-trapped left, over centuries, to recognise the existence and potential of this spiritual alchemy has had terrible consequences. Humanity continues to drive itself mad with its pursuit of external pleasures that have no power whatsoever to deliver internal peace and bliss. The mind *cannot* be appeased in this way, the wheel of *samsara* will keep on turning. The attempt is guaranteed to fail, exactly as it is guaranteed to consume the natural world on which we depend for our survival.

Head-trapped political activists can continue to devote themselves to struggling with global problems rooted in insatiable greed and egotism, but nothing much will change as long as our hearts remain the same.

Until we learn to face, observe and transmute our desires — to experience the love and bliss buried beneath thought, within pain — we will continue to be seduced by the fiery promises of desire for more, more and ever more. No amount of political awareness of the destructive impact of unrestrained greed will be able to dissuade people for whom too much can never be enough.

1. Aryadeva Gyel-tsap, *Yogic Deeds of Bodhisattvas*, Snow Lion, 1994, pp.120–1.
2. Leo Tolstoy, *Writings On Civil Disobedience and Non-Violence*, New Society, 1987, p.109.
3. Osho, *I Say Unto You, Volume 2 — Talks on the Sayings of Jesus*, Diamond Pocket Books, 2000, p.138. https://oshoworld.com/wp-content/uploads/2020/11/ebooks/English/061_I_Say_Unto_You_Vol2.pdf.
4. *The Seven Samurai*, cited, IMDB. https://www.imdb.com/title/tt0047478/quotes/?item=qt2872049&ref_=ext_shr_lnk.
5. Wayne, cited, IMDB. https://www.imdb.com/title/tt0053221/quotes/?item=qt0346740&ref_=ext_shr_lnk.
6. Tolle, *The Power Of Now*, Hodder & Stoughton, 2001, p.185.
7. Michael Singer, *The Untethered Soul — The Journey Beyond Yourself*, New Harbinger, 2007, p.105.
8. Robert Adams, *Silence of the Heart — Dialogues With Robert Adams*, Acropolis Books, 1999, pp.9–10.
9. Ananta, quoted, Steve Taylor, *Extraordinary Awakenings — When Trauma Leads to Transformation*, New World Library, 2021, ebook version, pp.64–65.

10. Ananta, cited, ibid., p.65.
11. Joseph Campbell with Bill Moyers, *The Power of Myth*, Doubleday, 1988, p.120.
12. *True Happiness This Way Lies*, from the album *Dusk*, The The, 1993. https://www.azlyrics.com/lyrics/thethe/truehappinessthiswaylies.html.
13. *Out of The Blue (Into The Fire)*, from the album *Infected*, The The, 1986.
14. *Bluer Than Midnight*, from the album *Dusk*, The The, 1993.
15. Master Yagyu, quoted, Osho, *The Path of Paradox, Volume 1*, Osho International Foundation, 1981, p.122.
16. Montaigne, John Gross (ed.), *The Oxford Book of Aphorisms*, Oxford University Press, 1983, p.172.
17. Alfred Bloom (ed.), *The Shin Buddhist Classical Tradition Volume 2: A Reader in Pure Land Teaching*, World Wisdom, 2014, p.111.
18. Lama Zopa Rinpoche, *Ultimate Healing*, Wisdom Publications, 2001, p.33.
19. *Eckhart Tolle Now* website, December 2020. https://members.eckharttolle.com/.

Chapter 4

Misdirected — Looking in the Wrong Direction

Loving bliss is real, it exists as the inherent nature of every human being. It is the answer to the human condition, to the great human crisis. It is an awakening from 'the nightmare of history'. No matter how lost in delusion, no matter how 'fallen' we may appear to be, our loving bliss remains — it cannot be destroyed or tarnished. It can only be obscured.

Eastern mythology is full of man-eating giants, human monsters lost in violence and delusion, and their dramatic encounters with spiritual masters at or past the point of enlightenment. The message, endlessly repeated, is that no matter how depraved, the seemingly 'evil' mind is just a whirling cloud of thoughts conditioned by the family, friends and society around us. The thought-droplets making up this toxic cloud can be evaporated by focusing attention on physical sensations and emotions, unveiling a hidden source of love that dissolves even the most destructive, poisonous ego.

Everybody — you, me, every tyrant, every criminal — is a dust-covered Buddha in need of attentional polishing. We are all beset by a dream-like fog of thoughts for which we are not to blame, and which can be dispersed.

But if this loving bliss is real, if it truly *is* the answer, how is it possible that so few people are aware that it exists? How can so many people be completely nonplussed by the claim that it *does* exist? And why is it almost never discussed, even by people who have experienced it?

The answer is that the human mind, individually and collectively through social institutions, has an awesome capacity to filter out and ignore what really matters. Political analyst Noam Chomsky said it best:

> The basic principle, rarely violated, is that what conflicts with the requirements of power and privilege does not exist.[1]

Powerful political and cultural forces persuade us to ignore our inner reality as non-existent and to direct our gaze outside to the supposed happiness and success that can be found in wealth, fame and high-status consumption.

It's not difficult to imagine what corporations would make of the idea that their products and services are mere rocks and pebbles beside the diamonds and pearls of loving bliss that fall into our lap when we sit doing (and buying) *nothing*.

'Mainstream' indifference is not the result of a conspiracy; it's the result of trial and error following the path of least resistance to profit. Writer Alan Durning described the underlying worldview:

> Even if they fail to sell a particular product, they sell consumerism itself by ceaselessly reiterating the idea that there is a product to solve each of life's problems, indeed that existence would be satisfying and complete if only we bought the right things.[2]

Retailing analyst Victor Lebow indicated the level of fanaticism involved:

> Our enormously productive economy … demands that we make consumption our way of life, that we convert the buying and use of goods into rituals, that we seek spiritual satisfaction, our ego satisfaction, in consumption … We

> need things, consumed, burned up, worn out, replaced, and discarded at an ever-increasing rate.[3]

We don't hear about, or experience, loving bliss in meditation because the world around us encourages us to view the search for internal solutions as a nonsensical, weird, almost masturbatory form of self-indulgence. The levels of confusion and distortion are out of this world and long-lived.

One hundred years ago, Somerset Maugham described an encounter with an English meditator in India:

> He said that he was fortunate in that he was one of the few persons who had a real desire and liking for meditation; and that he had always practised it ... But I could not get from him exactly what he meant by meditation. I could not understand if he was actively thinking of a certain subject ... It was hard to make up one's mind what sort of a man he was. He was certainly very happy. I had thought to discover something of the truth about him from what he looked like and from what he said, but I came away completely puzzled.[4]

One hundred years later, Western writers remain 'completely puzzled'. In his book *Humankind*, an exploration of the thesis that 'most people, deep down, are pretty decent', historian, Rutger Bregman wrote:

> To be honest, I gave meditating a shot, but it hasn't been a huge success so far. For some reason there's always another email, another tweet or another video of a goat on a trampoline demanding immediate attention.[5]

It is remarkable that an author exploring the fundamental benevolence of human beings has not seriously experimented with meditation, and therefore has no experience of the loving bliss found in meditation.

Misdirected 1 — The Failure of External 'Success'

Sitting for an hour a day watching our sensations, thoughts and feelings would appear to be entirely doable. But the overwhelming and relentless emphasis of our society is that we should be focused outside ourselves. In Chapter 2, we discussed Kabir's advice:

> Don't go outside your house to see flowers, my friend, don't bother with that excursion. Inside your body there are flowers. One flower has a thousand petals.[6]

The claim: not just happiness, but ecstasy, is found *inside*, not outside.

But are we really to believe that we should not 'bother with' hardcore external 'success' — big stuff like global fame, historic achievement and unrestrained indulgence?

Consider the thrill and fame of record-breaking adventure. Climber Joe Simpson described his feelings on being part of the first ever team to summit *Siula Grande* in the Peruvian Andes by the West face:

> We took the customary summit photos and ate some chocolate. I felt the usual anticlimax. What now? It was a vicious circle. If you succeed with one dream, you come back to square one and it's not long before you're conjuring up another, slightly harder, a bit more ambitious — a bit more dangerous. I didn't like the thought of where it might be leading me.[7]

Conjuring up another dream, Simpson later went through hell when he was seriously injured and very nearly died on the same mountain.

Or consider the success of a writer we've just mentioned, Somerset Maugham. In his book, *Conversations With Willie*, nephew Robin Maugham described his uncle, 'Willie' (Somerset Maugham), as 'certainly the most famous author alive. And he was probably the saddest'.[8] The elder Maugham had indeed exceeded the wildest dreams of any author:

> At the age of ninety-one my uncle ... still made a fortune – even though he had not written a word for ages. The royalties from his books and short stories still literally flowed in from all over the world. And so did the fan-letters: he got more than three hundred a week – most of them from teenagers ...
>
> At this moment four of his plays were running in Germany. His play *The Circle* had been brilliantly revived in England ... and *The Constant Wife* had just been turned into a musical. One of his most famous novels, *Of Human Bondage*, was soon to be made into a film – which might bring him as many millions of dollars as did *Rain*, *The Moon and Sixpence* and *The Razor's Edge*.
>
> Unfortunately, the one reward all Willie's talent and success had not given him was happiness.[9]

Maugham, it seems, 'would shuffle through the vast, deserted rooms' of his luxurious villa on Cap Ferrat in the South of France 'like a lost ghost':

> He sought comfort in the past. He was bewildered by the present, and afraid of the future.[10]

He had 11 servants and ate off silver plates, 'But it no longer meant anything to him'.[11]

Maugham's nephew asked him: 'What is the happiest memory of your life?'

Maugham stammered in reply: 'I cer-can't think of a single moment.'[12]

His nephew asked again:

> You're the most famous writer alive. Surely that means something?[13]

He replied:

> I wish I'd never written a single word. It's brought me nothing but misery... Everyone who's got to know me well has ended up by hating me ... My whole life has been a failure ... And now it's too late to change. It's too late.[14]

Robin Maugham commented:

> I looked round the drawing-room at the immensely valuable furniture and pictures and objects that Willie's success had enabled him to acquire. I remembered that the villa itself and the wonderful garden I could see through the windows — a fabulous setting on the edge of the Mediterranean — were worth six hundred thousand pounds [equivalent to around £2.5 million now].[15]

As this suggests, great wealth has no ability to deliver great happiness. (See Howard C. Cutler's *The Art of Happiness* and Tim Kasser's *The High Price of Materialism* for discussion and statistical evidence.)

Millionaire, Karl Rabeder, provided an interesting insight into the problem of fakery that surrounds wealth:

> It was 1998, and my wife and I went to Hawaii for three weeks and spent an enormous amount of money. We said,

> OK, we're going to have a perfect holiday, only five-star hotels and helicopter flying and whatever. And we really had the feeling there were no real people in this kind of life — *it's just actors playing the role of being happy*. And I decided I didn't want to be part of this thing.[16]

Perhaps scaling literal and literary mountains, and piles of money, doesn't really cut it. Perhaps, instead, we should focus on genuinely mind-blowing, historic achievements. Consider the case of Apollo astronaut, Buzz Aldrin, for example.

Having travelled 250,000 miles from his home planet and having waited 20 minutes for the other guy to get down the ladder, Aldrin became the second person to walk on the moon on 21 July 1969.

Back on Earth, 600 million people looked up in wonder: how did it feel to be the first humans ever to set foot on another world? That surely *must* have delivered an overwhelming sense of success. After all, Aldrin and Neil Armstrong were globally perceived as the ultimate pioneers at the cutting edge of human progress — if anyone was really living life to the full, they were. So how *did* it feel to be up there 'living the dream' of external 'success'? Aldrin recalled of his return to Earth:

> I said to Neil, 'We missed the whole thing.' We didn't share the moment of exhilaration here on Earth. We were sort of out of town doing something else.[17]

A remarkable comment that recalls Lama Zopa Rinpoche's observation:

> There is always something missing. If you examine your mind in everyday life, you can see that something is missing all the time ... You are never really happy.[18]

Perhaps we can recognise this from our own lives, but it is pretty amazing that it was also true of Aldrin's experience of moonwalking. He described the moon as a scene of 'magnificent desolation' but, tellingly, added that the words also 'seemed to describe my own inner turmoil'.[19] Why?

> What's left? I wondered. What's a person do when his or her greatest dreams and challenges have been achieved? I reached over to the small table next to the chaise and reached for my drink, Scotch poured generously over ice cubes.[20]

This, of course, echoes Joe Simpson's 'What now?' comment above, and also the marvellous encounter between Emperor Alexander the Great and the mystic Diogenes. Travelling with his army to India to complete his global conquest, Alexander was advised that he would be passing a sage who lived naked in a barrel by a river without so much as a bowl for his food.

We can imagine the mighty emperor strolling down to the river, with his sceptical entourage no doubt equally amused and annoyed that their leader had to go to a beggar, rather than the other way around. In the event, Alexander was deeply impressed by the grace, beauty and dignity of this curious individual who, on hearing the announcement, 'Alexander the Great is coming!', laughed:

> Anyone who declares that he is great, cannot be![21]

Diogenes asked:

> Are you satisfied with conquering so many lands?

Alexander replied:

> No, unless I conquer the whole world I will not be satisfied.

Diogenes laughed again:

> Remember my words. Even if you conquer the whole world, your mind will ask for more, and there is no other world to conquer. Remember … you have conquered the world that is, and there is no other world to conquer — and mind is asking for more. You will be in such a frustration that you cannot conceive of it right now.

Alexander shrugged off the comment and continued on his way. But he had been shaken to the core by the meeting — he remembered Diogenes. Indeed, at the time of his death, Alexander instructed that his hands should be left hanging out of the funeral casket to show that he had left the world empty-handed, frustrated, exactly as Diogenes had predicted.

Like Aldrin, 'conqueror' of the moon, Alexander had found only emptiness and frustration in ultimate 'triumph' — there was 'always something missing'. Worse followed for the astronaut:

> Guilt and despair began to envelop me … How could I have gone almost overnight from being on top of the world to feeling useless, worthless and washed up? … There was no goal, no sense of calling, no project worth pouring myself into … Life seemed to have lost its lustre. On some days I couldn't even find a reason to get out of bed. So I didn't. Something was wrong; something within me was beginning to crack. I only hoped I could figure it out before I broke down completely.[22]

Aldrin wrote:

> I always enjoyed challenging people to think beyond the stars, to reach for their own 'moon' or 'outer space', whatever that might imply for them. Yet for me personally, by the autumn of 1970, there was a growing frustration and anxiousness at the center of my being that I could not resolve.[23]

He added ominously:

> A volcano was seething within me, below the surface of my life, the pressure building more each passing week. The only relief I found was in another shot of Scotch — and then another.[24]

Ultimately, Aldrin's family broke up, he married again, divorced again, and continued to hit the bottle. In 1972, he was hospitalised for a month for treatment and therapy for depression. Tragicomically, just eight years after the tickertape parades, the renowned moonwalker could be found working at a Cadillac dealership in Beverly Hills, where he failed to sell a single car. His comment:

> You get a job as a car salesman and you're a horrible car salesman. What does that do to a person's ego?[25]

Aldrin quoted Carl Jung:

> Space flights are merely an escape, a fleeing away from oneself, because it is easier to go to Mars or the moon than it is to penetrate one's own being.[26]

How about ultimate sporting success? On 30 July 1966, having had beans on toast and a pot of tea for lunch, England footballer, Geoff Hurst, took to the pitch at Wembley football stadium and scored a hat-trick to win the World Cup final against West Germany. It was an historic, iconic triumph that, if anything, resonates even more powerfully as the years go by. And yet, in his autobiography, Hurst wrote:

> There was a tremendous feeling of anti-climax when we [the team] got home. The whole thing had passed so quickly ... I cut the lawn because I hadn't been home for ages. Then I washed the car. It was pretty much like any other Sunday afternoon. I was a national hero but I didn't feel like one.
>
> It might sound a bit pretentious, but for me it had been another football match, albeit a very important one ... When you are out there on the pitch, doing the job, you focus on the game and are not aware of the enormity of the occasion for other people. It's just like another day at the office. People may find that hard to believe but that's how I recall it, and so do many of my teammates at the time.[27]

Like Aldrin and Armstrong, they missed the whole thing!

But perhaps this emphasis on high-status 'success' is beside the point. Perhaps *real* external happiness is found in fantastic levels of self-indulgence.

Growing up in the 1970s, I watched pop idol David Cassidy rise to fame on the BBC's *Top of the Pops*, in newspapers, and in numerous teen magazines, adored by millions of young girls, my big sister included. Surely Cassidy was 'living the dream'! After all, as he wrote in his autobiography:

> I never had to hit on women. I didn't have to. Women would come up to me all the time and say things like, 'Hi, want to have sex with me?' ... Sex was just sex. It was there. It presented itself to me numerous times during

> the course of the day, and I could take advantage of it or not. Pick anyone. Who would you like to meet? Who would you like to sleep with? I was 21 years old, I was always ready, and they were all so willing. Yeah, I can live with this ... The most beautiful women in the world were calling me, saying, 'I've got to see you. Please let me see you'. And they would come up to my room.[28]

Perhaps dying a little inside, one of Cassidy's friends commented:

> It used to astonish me the power of fame and celebrity, and what women would subject themselves to. They might be in a committed relationship, they might be married, and they would throw themselves at him. For a one-nighter they were going to just throw their morals right out of the window. The number of women used to astonish me.[29]

A number indicated by the fact that Cassidy received between 20,000 to 30,000 fan letters a week. He commented:

> Once the show went on the air, it became hard for me even to get into the studio in the morning. In the fall of 1970, there'd routinely be 40 or 50 fans crowding the entrance. Some of the more aggressive girls would bare their breasts, some would follow me while I drove home after working all day. There were girls who'd spend days and nights outside the studio, some even sleeping there.[30]

There was a hitch:

> I was particularly bothered by my inability to form lasting friendships with women.[31]

This is a common theme, of course. Nina Persson had her moment of global fame in the 1990s as singer with the Swedish band, The Cardigans. She found fame a bewildering and lonely experience. Persson said of a close relationship at this time:

> It was pretty much a catastrophe. He was with me only because I was famous, but he was terribly jealous of me, and always insecure. We lasted a year somehow, a horrible time. I was successful, making a lot of money, and I enjoyed none of it.[32]

This is the same jealousy expressed by Gore Vidal and suffered by John McEnroe, as discussed in Chapter 1. Cassidy had the same problem:

> My friends were brutal about me being in the teen magazines. They laughed at me and tortured me beyond belief. To them, I was a joke.[33]

He experienced fame as a kind of imprisonment:

> With all the publicity exposure, it became impossible for me to go in a store or even walk down a street without being stopped by people. At first, I enjoyed the sheer novelty of having fans. Quickly I began to sense problems ahead.[34]

Actress Emma Mackey, who played the character 'Maeve' in the hit series *Sex Education*, made the point that fans are obsessed with someone other than the actor themselves:

> I don't think anyone gives a shit about celebrities ... they don't care about me. It's Maeve, it's not necessarily me.

> They don't know me. So, what does it actually mean? Celebrityism, or whatever, is a byproduct of the job. I certainly didn't get into acting to become a celebrity, because it's terrifying. You'd have to be a complete sociopath to want to be a celebrity ... I find it absurd.[35]

Film 'star' Kevin Bacon described his experience of becoming famous:

> There's no way to describe fame, or all that attention, to anyone who hasn't experienced it. It's not just the fact that everyone knows you, it's something different. A nightmare.[36]

Paul Newman, one of the most renowned film 'stars', sounded a stark warning:

> Nobody can come to respect and love their anonymity until they've lost it.[37]

Justine Frischmann of rock band Elastica, who had her 15 minutes of fame in the 1990s, expanded on the nature of the problem:

> It invades every area of your life and makes you paranoid in a really peculiar way. It takes the spontaneity away. I always thought being famous would bring me freedoms and I suddenly realised that the opposite was true, that when you have people peering into your life, you have to really, really watch your step. And live in a very closed way. You have to be very careful of voicing any opinions or doing anything that people might disapprove of ...[38]

Six months into broadcasting *The Partridge Family*, the TV sitcom that made him famous, Cassidy contacted the publisher and owner of several teen magazines focusing on him and the show:

> I went into the office and said, 'I can't live like this anymore. I want you to take me out of your magazines. Take me off your covers'. And he looked at me and laughed, in a kind sort of way.[39]

What might have looked like heaven from the outside, quickly became a hell:

> There were times, during my tours, when I was afraid for my life, because I saw fans turn into a mob, and a mob can't easily be controlled … they didn't want to kill me — but their emotions were at fever pitch. And they all wanted a piece of me.[40]

Before the end of the first season of the TV show, things started to go seriously wrong:

> … my body began breaking down from overwork … I had serious problems with my gall bladder. At just 21 years old, I was one of the youngest patients the doctors said they'd ever seen with that problem.[41]

As for life as a pop 'star':

> No matter how pleasurable it might be for that one hour of the day when you were performing on stage, the other 23 hours of the day were impossible to cope with. They were hell.[42]

Poignantly, Cassidy recounted the time he met Elvis Presley:

> There was a sadness about Elvis that I recognised in myself. He too surrounded himself with friends. I knew all about the hysteria and madness he had gone through. So we had a unique sort of connection …
>
> Meeting Elvis that time was like seeing myself ten or fifteen years from then, sad and lonely. I couldn't get it out of my head.[43]

Once again, echoing Lama Zopa, something was missing:

> Even though there were millions of people who loved me and worshipped me and wanted me, I needed something more.[44]

Like Aldrin, wishing he could have watched the moon landings from Earth, the 'more' that Cassidy wanted was actually *less*:

> I began to envy my old high-school classmates who'd gone on to college. I even envied people with 'normal' jobs. Either of these paths seemed preferable to the one I'd taken. I started longing to have any other career but my own. It may sound absurd now, but it's true. There I was, rich and famous, a star, wishing at times I could be some thoroughly ordinary, anonymous guy instead. I'd dream about what it would be like to work at a real man's job.[45]

Misdirected 2 — Head-Trapped Intellectuals

Powerful economic, political and cultural interests rooted in the human ego naturally wage a propaganda war in favour of the idea that happiness must be sought externally.

This industrial system is itself a manifestation of an intellectual tradition deeply rooted in the seventeenth- and eighteenth-century European Enlightenment. The *philosophes* declared that humanity could rely on reason, notably the scientific method, to transform the external world in unending 'progress'. Reason was everything, with feeling dismissed as an irrelevance, at best; at worst, a corrupting influence undermining reason.

Historically then, our entire intellectual culture has been steadfastly head-trapped. Contempt awaits anyone who suggests that feeling is not only *not* a threat to reason, is not merely a complement to reason, but is actually *the great empowering and protective support for reason*. The irony is that it is only the loving bliss experienced in meditation that has the power to counter the fantastically distorting effect on reason supplied by our three friends, the Successful, Suffering and Righteous Egos.

As discussed in Chapter 2, thinking blocks feeling. Intense overthinking almost completely obstructs access to the innate love and bliss inside us.

To be blocked from an authentic feeling of being, is to be dead inside. The ego will enjoy cardboard adventures in 'achievement', attention and applause, but our hearts will be a wasteland. We will have transient pleasure but no ecstasy. We read, above, of how Somerset Maugham 'would shuffle through the vast, deserted rooms' of his luxurious villa in the South of France 'like a lost ghost', seeking 'comfort in the past ... bewildered by the present, and afraid of the future'.

The past is dead, non-existential; it exists only in the mind as a thought-based facsimile. The same is true of the future. To seek comfort in the past is to be dead, head-trapped; disconnected from the present, from feeling, from the heart. This is indeed to live as a ghost inhabiting a non-existential realm of the imagination.

A head-trapped person receives an affectionate touch like an electric shock. It's painful; it reminds them of how tense, how like a brain in a jar they have become.

Some of our most celebrated and 'successful' intellectuals have openly described the suffering of the head-trapped life. They have sometimes even managed to battle through their torment to perceive the nature of the problem and the beginnings of a solution.

Charles Darwin wrote in his autobiography:

> My mind has changed during the last twenty or thirty years ... Now for many years I cannot endure to read a line of poetry ... I have also almost lost any taste for pictures or music ... My mind seems to have become a kind of machine for grinding general laws out of large collections of facts ...[46]

Darwin suffered from numerous anxieties, breakdowns and depressions, as well as psychosomatic and other illnesses. Biographer John Bowlby wrote:

> Darwin had a strong tendency to respond to adversity with both acute and chronic anxiety and sometimes also with depression. Note, for example, the revealing phrase inserted into the detailed account of his somatic symptoms: 'hysterical crying'.[47]

Darwin used intellectual work as a kind of anti-meditation to repress his feelings. Bowlby commented:

> Work was constantly used by Darwin as a means of diverting his attention from his bodily discomforts and also, as he frequently insists, from thoughts about whatever was causing him anxiety or depression. Time and time again in his letters he refers to the anaesthetic effects of work. When not yet forty he writes to his wife:

> 'I was speculating yesterday how fortunate it was I had plenty of employment ... for being employed alone makes me forget myself.' Ten years later, on 4 February 1861, after telling his close friend Joseph Hooker that he is 'never comfortable except at work', he adds: 'the word "holiday" is written in a dead language for me, and much do I grieve it'. During his mid-fifties, in 1864 and 1865, he writes in similar vein to no fewer than three of his regular correspondents...[48]

This attests to the tremendous power of thought to block feeling, to 'forget myself'.

Darwin clearly understood the price he had paid for his head-trapped life:

> If I had to live my life again, I would have made a rule to read some poetry and listen to some music at least once every week ... The loss of these tastes is a loss of happiness, and may possibly be injurious to the intellect, and more probably to the moral character, by enfeebling the emotional part of our nature.[49]

Far better even than poetry would have been an hour a day spent watching his thoughts, sensations and feelings. But as we have seen, this kind of meditation was a far-distant prospect for nineteenth-century intellectuals.

Earlier, we mentioned John Stuart Mill, the most influential English-speaking philosopher of his time. Raised by his philosopher father to be an intellectual prodigy, at age 3 he was taught Greek. By the age of 8, he had studied far more Greek literature and British history than was good for him, as well as arithmetic, physics and astronomy. Unsurprisingly, Mill, too, soon plunged into darkness. Aged just 20, deep depression caused him to consider suicide. He had identified his happiness with a huge, head-trapped goal:

> I had what might truly be called an object in life; to be a reformer of the world. My conception of my own happiness was entirely identified with this object.[50]

One day, inevitably, his belief that this grandiose ambition could bring him happiness fell apart:

> But the time came when I awakened from this as from a dream.[51]

Mill had asked himself:

> Suppose that all your objects in life were realized; that all the changes in institutions and opinions which you are looking forward to, could be completely effected at this very instant: would this be a great joy and happiness to you?
>
> And an irrepressible self-consciousness distinctly answered, 'No!' At this my heart sank within me: the whole foundation on which my life was constructed fell down. All my happiness was to have been found in the continual pursuit of this end. The end had ceased to charm, and how could there ever again be any interest in the means? I seemed to have nothing left to live for.[52]

Mill confessed that these lines in Coleridge's *Dejection* 'exactly describe my case':

> A grief without a pang, void, dark, and drear,
> A stifled, drowsy, unimpassioned grief,

> Which finds no natural outlet or relief,
> In word, or sigh, or tear.[53]

Even the prospect of a 'just society', an earthly paradise, could not make Mill happy because it was rooted in mere ideals, ideas. He was head-trapped in a dead dream of the future to such an extent that he was completely disconnected from his heart in the living present, the only place and time happiness can be found and felt.

A 'moral success' delivers no more happiness to a heart blocked by overthinking than any other type of external 'success'. The head, actually the ego, may feel a thin, short-lived satisfaction from achieving its goals. But the pleasure lasts an instant and is followed by a fall into the emptiness predicted by Diogenes and experienced by Alexander. So you conquer the whole world, so you 'conquer' the highest mountain, so you sell a million books, so you sleep with a million women, so you create a just society: So what?! What's next?

The answer: nothing, just bleak emptiness, because the answer is found in the heart, not in the head. The only thing 'next' is more of the same, with ever-diminishing returns followed by the same abysmal 'desolation', no matter how 'magnificent'. 'Next' is non-existential; we can wander there only as lost souls, as ghosts.

Like Darwin, Mill discovered a remedy for his torment:

> I had now learnt by experience that the passive susceptibilities [feeling] needed to be cultivated as well as the active capacities [intellect], and required to be nourished and enriched as well as guided ... *The cultivation of the feelings became one of the cardinal points in my ethical and philosophical creed.*[54]

Mill found he was best able to reawaken his feelings through poetry:

> What made Wordsworth's poems a medicine for my state of mind, was that they expressed, not mere outward beauty, but states of feeling, and of thought coloured by feeling, under the excitement of beauty. They seemed to be the very culture of the feelings, which I was in quest of. In them I seemed to draw from a source of inward joy, of sympathetic and imaginative pleasure ...[55]

Over and over again, Mill talks of feeling — he needed *to feel,* to escape from the tyranny of his mind.

The head-trapped intellectualism that tortured Darwin and Mill is all around us. Over decades and centuries, this has casually dismissed the idea that there might be some inner world worth exploring. The evolutionary biologist, Richard Dawkins, has gone so far as to write:

> We are survival machines — robot vehicles blindly programmed to preserve the selfish molecules known as genes. This is a truth which still fills me with astonishment.[56]

What on earth could blindly programmed, molecule-serving 'robot vehicles' hope to gain from observing their automaton feelings through gaps in the mechanical chains of thought? The bliss and love that meditators claim to experience must be some kind of genetically selfish delusion; a bizarre attempt to polish the mechanical turd of life lived as 'survival machines'. We must surely cringe in revulsion at any suggestion that there might be something to be attained by looking 'within'. Such nonsense! Are we to believe we are any less mechanical within than without?

In reality, Dawkins' 'robot vehicles' comment carries meaningful echoes of Darwin's lament:

> My mind seems to have become a kind of machine for grinding general laws out of large collections of facts...

The head-trapped intellectual *is* indeed a kind of 'machine'; a kind of blind 'robot', disconnected from love and bliss.

Nobody who has heard a single note of Kabir's 'divine melody' could be so tone deaf to the utter, glittering mystery of this universe and the consciousness that perceives it. Dawkins' dismal judgement is closer to psychological projection than Truth.

Brain in a Jar — The Break Out!

In 2015, Amy Goodman of *Democracy Now!* interviewed the world's leading political activist, Noam Chomsky, one of my own great inspirations, on the happy event of his remarrying at the ripe age of 86. This was a fascinating, because rare, example of a leading figure on the left actually being asked to say something about love. Specifically, Chomsky was asked why he had said, 'Life without love is empty'.[57]

Chomsky is famous for never failing to surprise his questioners with some startling new insight, some hidden angle exposing false assumptions in the question. His response on this occasion was shocking because he added nothing at all:

> Well, I could produce some clichés which have the merit of being true — a life without love is a pretty empty affair. It's a...

It wasn't that Chomsky had been interrupted; his voice simply trailed away as if he didn't know what more to say. He had already indicated his lack of enthusiasm for this line of questioning when he commented: 'I have always been a very private person'.

But the issue of love, the emptiness of a life without love, is about far more than private romance. In fact, it is a crucial subject about which Chomsky has never had anything significant to say. And he is not alone. I'm focusing on this tiny exchange because he is our most influential dissident, but also because I'm not aware of any other contemporary, high-profile leftist having discussed the issue at all.

By contrast, psychologist, Erich Fromm, cut a lonely figure on the left in the 1970s, when he wrote:

> I believe that love is the main key to open the doors to the 'growth' of man. Love and union with someone or something outside of oneself, union that allows one to put oneself into relationship with others, to feel one with others, without limiting the sense of integrity and independence...
>
> I believe that the experience of love is the most human and humanising act that is given to man to enjoy and that it, like reason, makes no sense if conceived in a partial way.[58]

But even this only scratches the surface. First of all, what *is* love? How does love as romantic attachment — the impassioned need for another — relate to love as an urge to share with and care for others? And what is the relationship between love and reason? While romantic attachment inhibits reason ('love is blind'), compassionate love neutralises this filtering effect of desire.

And what about the problem of love and ego? As discussed in Chapter 1, when we help others, we place ourselves in a position of superiority over them. And what about the relationship between love and the craving for attention that is such a central feature of the ego?

So why don't left progressives talk about these issues? Why don't they talk about love and sex? Why don't they talk about desire, about human emotions in general (other than anger and 'concern for others')?

In an interview, Chomsky was asked:

> The spiritual life in terms of religion. Is that at all a factor [in your life]?[59]

Chomsky replied:

> For, me, it's not. I am a child of the Enlightenment. I think irrational belief is a dangerous phenomenon, and I try consciously to avoid irrational belief.

The European Enlightenment certainly, and quite rightly, rejected irrational religious belief. Other legacies of the Enlightenment, though, have been disastrous. Rutger Bregman writes that Enlightenment thinkers believed that human beings had:

> one phenomenal talent ... a saving grace that sets us apart from other living creatures ... Reason.[60]

Bregman emphasises the point:

> Not empathy, or emotion, or faith. Reason. If Enlightenment philosophers put their faith in something, it was in the power of rational thought.
> Not empathy, or emotion ... Reason.

As discussed, reason was everything, with feeling dismissed as a corrupting influence.

Certainly, Chomsky would embrace 'empathy', but the prioritisation of reason over feeling has always been at the heart of political activism inspired by the Enlightenment — that is, virtually all socialism and anarchism.

Not just feelings, leftists typically reject discussion of all 'personal issues' as a distraction from the effort to generate political change. Even talk about personal experiences that would be of real value to other activists treading a similar path is rejected as self-indulgence.

When Chomsky was asked about an early childhood experience that encouraged him to back the underdog (he said he had witnessed an act of bullying but failed to stand up for the victim), he responded:

> That was a personal thing for me, I don't know why it should interest anyone.[61]

Asked how he can discuss such depressing political material year after year without burning out, he replied:

> I could talk to you about my personal reactions, but again I don't see why they should interest anyone.[62]

His underlying point is that his (and by implication, our) personal problems are so miniscule compared to those suffered by the victims of war and tyranny, that time spent on his own suffering is an embarrassing indulgence.

It is hardly a surprise, then — as I know from three decades of bruising personal experience — that left activists react to words like 'love', 'compassion', 'meditation' and 'loving bliss' like vampires to garlic. The cringe on social media is palpable.

To cite one typical example repeated countless times, a reader on the left-wing US website, *ZNet*, responded like this to one of my articles on meditation:

> WTF [What The Fuck]? ... Let's keep navel-gazing at a respectful distance.

In fact, to watch feelings in the heart and near the navel (three finger-widths below the navel, to be precise) — the latter, called the *'hara'* by Japanese Buddhists and 'the lower *dantian*' by Chinese Taoists — is the supreme antidote to the tyranny of the ego that is the ultimate cause of our political woes. This, though, is what the dictionary has to say:

> Definition of navel-gazing: useless or excessive self-contemplation.[63]

And these are the suggested synonyms:

> egocentricity, egocentrism, egoism, egomania, egotism, narcissism, self-absorption, self-centeredness, self-concern, self-interest, self-involvement, self-preoccupation, self-regard, selfishness, selfness.

Remarkably then, this common understanding that 'navel-gazing' is a sickly manifestation of egotism is an exact reversal of the truth.

The rejection of emotion and feeling is part of a general Western ethic of self-negation and self-sacrifice — we are to give our time, energy and strength *to help others*. This is viewed as an oppositional position to the 'mainstream', 'me-first' culture promoting self-indulgence and political indifference.

It is certainly true that 'mainstream' culture works hard to keep us focused on trivial personal issues — 'celebrity', makeovers, fashion — and away from more threatening political awareness. But the effort to turn within is anything but trivial. On the contrary, it is key to the task of becoming a mature, critical-thinking human being.

It is precisely by training us to *not* take our feelings seriously that we are made to subordinate those feelings to activities we instinctively revile: 'religious' self-repression, youth-crushing state education, soul-crushing corporate conformity, the obscenity of killing and being killed in the name of patriotic 'duty'.

If we have no ability to feel, understand and respect our feelings; if we have developed a fierce ability to override them, we have lost our capacity for emotional and intellectual self-defence. If what we feel doesn't matter, we will become victims of what we have been relentlessly *trained* to think by people who may not be working in our best interests.

Fromm described how modern men and women are trained to develop a 'marketing character'. These are people who view themselves as personality packages to be bought and sold on the job market, as cogs that should fit smoothly into the corporate machine.

Fromm noted that strong emotions like love and hate 'do not fit into a character structure that functions almost entirely on the cerebral level and avoids feelings, whether good or evil ones, because they interfere with the marketing character's main purpose: selling and exchanging'.[64] The result:

> ...they do not care, in any deep sense of the word, *not because they are so selfish but because their relations to others and to themselves are so thin*. This may also explain why they are not concerned with the dangers of nuclear and ecological catastrophes, even though they know all the data that points to these dangers.[65]

The truth is that political radicals reject issues related to feeling, not just because they believe it is an 'indulgence', but because, like Darwin and Mill, *they are themselves head-trapped intellectuals* who have similarly lost a taste for feeling, for all discussion of feeling.

By the way, I understand from my own experience why political activists react so strongly against words like 'love' and 'meditation'. It is a response that is not merely based on pragmatic fears of distraction from 'real issues'.

When I have been deeply head-trapped, working intensively on political writing, I *also* have tended to see talk about love, compassion and meditation as an irrelevance. That includes my *own* writing on these issues! This shift is a function of being head-trapped, of being blocked by a deep cloud of thought disconnecting us from emotions.

When we're intensely focused on intellectual work, talk of 'love' seems like some simpering nonsense from 'The Wonderful World of Disney' – pure saccharine. On the other hand, when we take a break from this overthinking, the smallest act of kindness, or the tender beauty of a child or an animal, can bring floods of tears as the repression is released.

As Somerset Maugham wrote:

> Sentimentality is only sentiment that rubs you up the wrong way.[66]

Away from the Colosseum of political debate, love and kindness, of course, *do not* seem childishly sentimental. Instead, it feels absurd to live as a flinty brain in a jar with an ice-cold, warrior heart. You will have noticed what a frigid, hostile place is X (formerly known as Twitter). It is a cauldron of dehumanised intellectual activity deprived of face-to-face human contact and emotional warmth.

The Enlightenment *philosophes* were wrong – reason is *not* neutral. Overthinking cuts us off from loving human emotions, from an ability to recognise their importance. One can be a brilliant, fair-minded, well-intentioned intellectual, and still cause immense harm. Laura Archera Huxley made the point well:

> ...not-love tends to beget not-love. The energy of love is needed to reconvert not-love into love.[67]

The problem is that intellectual analysis draws us ever deeper into thinking, which blocks feeling. It produces not-love, rather than love. It produces mere ideas *about* love which, ironically, block *real feelings* of love with the power to alchemise not-love into love.

When we think too much, feeling as such rubs us up the wrong way. By contrast, as discussed earlier, when tiny moments of ecstasy fall through gaps in thinking in meditation, we find ourselves able to hold, hug and kiss again. We become warm, loving humans in a way that intellectuals are conspicuously not.

And it is warm, loving humans that we need — people able to 'reconvert not-love into love'. In fact, they are not reconverting; they are not *doing* anything. Simple attention transforms the environment in our hearts from 'not-love into love'. And then, the simple presence of love in us can transform 'not-love into love' in other people. We are required to do nothing beyond creating an opening through which the 'fine rain' of love and bliss can be felt.

A world where feelings are *not* felt, understood and respected, is a world where numbed adults are easy meat for the crude stimulation and exploitation of agonising, bottled up desires, fears, guilt and aggression they are powerless to digest.

The standard aspiration is that head-trapped leftists might one day end up creating a peaceful, just world out of head-trapped but rational people who have little or no ability to understand, respect or experience their feelings.

But this is not possible. To be addicted, repressed and guilt-ridden is to be at war with oneself, with the rest of nature and with everyone else. Political activists have no option but to learn to discuss and deal with the issues of awareness and feeling. The 'private' *is*, quite obviously, political.

Jean-Jacques Rousseau – The Man with No Skin

The French philosopher, Jean-Jacques Rousseau, was a rare exception to the rule of Western head-trapped intellectuals. At a time when eighteenth-century Enlightenment thinkers were worshipping at the altar of the mind, Rousseau insisted that Truth was actually found in our hearts, in feeling. He wrote:

> ...good sense depends much more on the feelings of the heart than the brightness of the mind, and it is common experience that the most learned and enlightened people are not always those who conducted themselves best in the affairs of life.[68]

To this day, state education rejects this absolutely. No-one is interested in cultivating 'feelings of the heart'; children are evaluated according to 'the brightness of the mind'.

The Scottish philosopher, David Hume, who knew Rousseau well, described him as 'one of the most singular of all human beings ... his extreme sensibility of temper is his torment; he is like a man who were stripped not only of his clothes but of his skin'.[69]

Rousseau felt every pleasure, every pain, every delight and despair, deeply. It was this acuity of awareness that enabled him to uncover the hidden secrets of the human condition.

Two and a half centuries before 'mindfulness', Rousseau used the word *prévoyance*, 'foresight', 'to denote the habit of not living in the present moment but of thinking ahead', as historian John Hope Mason explained.[70] Rousseau wrote of this phenomenon:

> Foresight! Foresight which is ever bidding us look forward into the future, a future which in many cases we shall never reach. Here is the real source of all our troubles! How mad it is for so short-lived a creature as

> man to look forward into a future which he rarely attains, while he neglects the present which is his! ... *We no longer live where we are, but where we are not!*[71]

Rousseau understood that it is impossible to satisfy a mind that 'neglects the present', that values only what it does not have.

Quite wonderfully, Rousseau's final, unfinished work, *Reveries of The Solitary Walker*, written in the two years before his death in 1778, contains a simple guide to what amounts to *zazen* meditation (*'zazen'* sounds exotic but actually means 'just sitting, doing nothing', watching).

As clearly as any Eastern mystic, Rousseau described the inevitable failure of ordinary happiness that has been the theme of this chapter. Remarkably, he went so far as to suggest that none of us actually knows what happiness *is*:

> Thus our earthly joys are almost without exception the creatures of a moment; I doubt whether any of us knows the meaning of lasting happiness. Even in our keenest pleasures there is scarcely a single moment of which the heart could truthfully say: 'Would that this moment could last for ever!' And how can we give the name of happiness to a fleeting state which leaves our hearts still empty and anxious, either regretting something that is past or desiring something that is yet to come?[72]

We might like to conduct this thought experiment for ourselves! Looking back, is it not clear that even our happiest moments were tainted by fear of failure, change and loss? Yes, attainment of some 'object of desire' gives momentary pleasure, but our minds quickly latch onto some other person, experience or object 'yet to come', and desire reaches out into this new, alluring distance.

Simply by paying close attention to his suffering and happiness, the ultra-sensitive Rousseau discovered a joyfulness beyond the fantasies of a mind lost in *prévoyance*. Having given away his gold watch, Rousseau wrote:

> But if there is a state where the soul can find a resting-place secure enough *to establish itself and concentrate its entire being there, with no need to remember the past or reach into the future,* where time is nothing to it, where the present runs on indefinitely but this duration goes unnoticed, with no sign of the passing of time, and no other feeling of deprivation or enjoyment, pleasure or pain, desire or fear than the simple feeling of existence, a feeling that fills our soul entirely, as long as this state lasts, we can call ourselves happy, not with a poor, incomplete and relative happiness such as we find in the pleasures of life, but *with a sufficient, complete and perfect happiness which leaves no emptiness to be filled in the soul.* Such is the state which I often experienced in my solitary reveries on the Island of Saint-Pierre...[73]

After a lifetime of ambition, struggle and suffering, Rousseau had discovered the 'sufficient, complete and perfect happiness' of loving bliss. This revolutionary experience is available to any soul freed from thoughts of past and future and able to 'concentrate its entire being' in the present.

Epilogue: 'Burning Among Stars in the Night'

I travelled with my dad — 'H', as we called him — in the back seat of the car. It was the same way we'd driven a million times — to Tesco, to drop me off at the station, to drop me off at the airport, to drive up the M25 to my sister's at Christmas. It was a suitably cold, drizzly afternoon; our destination emptied of people by rain and virus.

Our tiny group trudged through the rain to a large oak tree, the designated spot. The whole place appeared to have been designed by computer. I took the plastic lid off the long cardboard tube, which was both disturbingly heavy and disturbingly light. I broke the paper seal and there was 'H' — as fine as flour, as white as rice — and I poured him in pluming, wind-blown arcs across the grass. There was a stiff breeze and I had to take care to avoid him being blown back over my new trainers.

Out of everything connected to my dad's death, this was the most surreal. That we found ourselves acting and speaking as though living, breathing, vibrant, chuckling, grumpy, boozy, Sudoku-filling, paper industry prodigy 'H' had become lifeless white ash sinking in semi-circular lines into cold wet grass on a grey September day.

Believing in Father Christmas is one thing, but to believe that a person is a pile of ash who somehow continues in that form! And yet we actually said things like, 'He'll be happy here under this oak tree' and 'Would you like to go and visit "H" under his tree?'

Family and friends seem to find nothing controversial in the frequently expressed hope, 'May he rest in peace', as though there is some doubt about the outcome. The suggestion, clearly, is that our loved one might *not* 'rest in peace'. The implication: they might become 'a restless spirit' — a ghost, no less; perhaps a zombie! In our age of (selective) political correctness, no-one seems to find this questionable.

Similarly, many of us seem to feel obligated to say, 'He passed'. Where to, 'the other side'? We're back among the ghosts! When a soap bubble bursts, did it 'pass', or did it cease to exist? Or we say, 'He passed away', to persuade ourselves that he is not dead at all — not even 'resting' — but has embarked on a mysterious journey, like Bilbo Baggins of Bag End. It doesn't help to be confronted by this delusion and denial at a time when the mind is already reeling.

On the other hand, it did help to know that my dad would have perceived the whole ash-scattering event as pointless. I remember him saying something like:

> I don't give a hoot what you do with me when I'm gone,
> I won't be there!

Indeed, even without the virus, it would have been difficult to have any kind of church 'service' knowing that the person being 'honoured' would have considered every aspect of the process a meaningless (and expensive!) farce exploiting minds less rational than his own. After the cremation, we played a selection of his favourite songs and had a drink. Did it 'honour the dead' to play *It's Not Unusual*, by fellow-Welshman Tom Jones?

That night, looking up at the ceiling in the pitch black of the room where he had died, I didn't 'honour' my dad, because I don't really know what that means, or why it's relevant in reference to the death of a loved one. I did find myself reflecting on Ernest Hemingway's version of honour and heroism, of 'grace under pressure' — an old fisherman battling sharks to save his prize catch; a civil war volunteer fighting a suicidal rear-guard action to save his comrades. It seemed to me that real heroism is more mundane.

Real heroism is trundling to and from Tesco every day, for years, in a little red car to do the shopping when you were once a shooting executive star. It's falling and cutting yourself horribly, because your 87-year-old skin is so thin, and just getting up and carrying on. It's carrying the empty bottles and rubbish down a flight of stone steps day after day because it has to be done, even though you've fallen many times in the house and falling down the steps would be fatal. It's losing every last one of your friends — until the village is empty of familiar faces and you are the longest-surviving member of your local club —

and just carrying on. Heroism is sitting on a sofa, day after day, watching daytime TV because there's not much else you can do, when you don't believe there's much point to anything anyway because you're an atheist, and just carrying on.

After my dad died, three related phenomena were clearly evident: a storm of thoughts in my head, a searing pool of emotional pain in my heart, and a witnessing consciousness observing both.

Here's a storm-chasing snapshot of my mind the night after he died. Without himself becoming infected, my dad had been stuck in a Covid-ridden hospital for the last four weeks of his life, unable to see any of us, communicating only by phone:

> 'I better go, Davy; I've got two scoops of ice cream waiting to be devoured. Bye!' My god, those were the last words he ever said to me! How on earth can he have died within 24 hours of being let out of hospital? Why did they let him go if he was so ill? They said his heart was at 25 per cent capacity, his kidneys same or worse. He had no idea if he was even on steroids. How will we take care of mum during the lockdown? She'll be alone in the house having lost her partner of 65 years. 65 years! And now she's alone at the age of 85! How must *that* feel?! How can we get medical help to her without her getting Covid? She almost fell over this morning because she hadn't slept. Are we going to lose both of them in the same month? 'Please, you can just pick me up and take me home — I've been stuck here for weeks; I can't take it anymore. Just take me home.' He must have been suffering horribly to say something like that. 'But there's no care package, if you just leave, H, you'll be on your own.' We should have just taken him out, we shouldn't have just left him there. How is it possible he could just die within 24 hours of being sent home? Will I end up being poured in white

> plumes across the crematorium grass? Who am I kidding? Of course I will! How will we take care of mum now? 'I've got two scoops of ice cream waiting to be devoured.' Mum's alone for the first time in 65 years! He said to her: 'Try to remember the good times.' How could he die the day after coming home?

And so on. This painful, endlessly cycling thought-storm was waiting for me in the treacherous wee small hours. As Rabindranath Tagore wrote so beautifully:

> Day's pain, muffled by its own glare
> burns among stars in the night.[74]

And this burning emotional pain was the second phenomenon: intense sadness, anxiety and anguish in the centre of my chest. This pain was, of course, provoked by thoughts. But the pain, in turn, fuelled more thoughts.

Surging thoughts, pain, and then a mysterious third phenomenon: my awareness, my consciousness, watching both. When this witnessing awareness focused on the thoughts in my head, they proliferated and the emotional pain in my chest intensified. By contrast, when the witness focused on the emotional pain, something different happened.

At first, the pain actually seemed to increase, because I was facing it directly for the first time. But as I continued to divert attention away from the thoughts to the pain, as I delved into the pain — feeling the sadness, the anguish as deeply as possible — my thoughts were deprived of the energy imparted by attention and started to subside. As the thinking subsided, so did the thought-driven pain in my chest. The more I focused on the painful feelings, the less energy was available to maintain either the thoughts or the pain.

Even this slight improvement was a relief, an encouragement. I continued to focus on the pain, which lessened even more. Thoughts continued to pop into my head, of course, but they now had less emotional suffering to feed off and so couldn't reinforce that pain so easily.

Eventually, it reached a point where I enjoyed feeling the pain; I didn't want to stop. In fact, I was no longer sure if it really was pain now. What was it, then: *pleasure?* In the immediate aftermath of my dad's death? It seemed almost indecent.

As the pain continued to reduce and thoughts lessened, a moment came when I was so focused on feeling that a tiny gap appeared in the chain of thoughts. Through that gap, a minute but intense point of bliss sparked in my chest. It was a blazing, ecstatic point of love and delight.

I focused attention on this tiny spark, which dissolved, spread and deepened, so that it formed a shimmering pool of bliss and love across my chest and upper back. It wasn't that I felt love for anyone in particular. Rather, love was there, and I felt love for whichever person popped into my thoughts, or for whatever object popped into my sense perceptions.

The burning anguish had now completely disappeared. I felt ecstatic delight, happiness, peace; I was overflowing with a loving warmth. This loving bliss — why not call it that rather than the tautological 'loving kindness', as if we're reluctant to admit we *feel* bliss? — stayed with me for the rest of the day. In reference to this experience, I made a short entry in my journal four days after my dad had died:

> Bliss in the afternoon meditation.

Emotional pain is ultimately driven by thought; when we stop focusing on thoughts and start focusing on perceptions, sensations and emotions, the thoughts subside. When a tiny gap eventually appears in the chain of thought, an internal source of love and bliss ordinarily obscured by mental activity is able to blaze through this gap in the clouds.

1. Noam Chomsky, *Deterring Democracy*, Hill and Wang, 1992, p.79.
2. Alan Durning, *How Much is Enough — The Consumer Society and the Future of the Earth*, Worldwatch Environmental Series, 1992, p.119.
3. Lebow, quoted Sharon Beder, *Global Spin — The Corporate Assault on Environmentalism*, Green Books, 1997, p.161.
4. W. Somerset Maugham, *A Writer's Notebook*, Penguin, 1993, p.252.
5. Rutger Bregman, *Humankind — A Hopeful History*, Bloomsbury, 2019, p.2 and p.388.
6. Kabir, cited, Robert Bly (trans.), *The Kabir Book: Forty-Four of the Ecstatic Poems of Kabir*, Boston: Beacon Press, 1977, p.47.
7. Joe Simpson, *Touching The Void*, Vintage, 1988, p.53.
8. Robin Maugham, *Conversations With Willie — Reflections of W. Somerset Maugham*, W. H. Allen, 1978, p.3.
9. Ibid., pp.3–4.
10. Ibid., p.3.
11. Ibid., p.4.
12. Ibid., p.4.
13. Ibid., p.6.
14. Ibid., p.7.
15. Ibid., p.7.
16. Simon Hattenstone, 'Who wants to be a millionaire?' in *The Guardian*, 5 June 2010; my emphasis. http://www.guardian.co.uk/society/2010/jun/05/millionaires-give-away-fortunes-philanthropy.
17. Aldrin, quoted, Robert Epstein, 'Buzz Aldrin: Down to Earth' in *Psychology Today*, 1 May 2001. https://www.

psychologytoday.com/us/articles/200105/buzz-aldrin-down-earth.

18. Lama Zopa Rinpoche, *Transforming Problems*, Wisdom Books, 1993, pp.30-31.
19. Buzz Aldrin, *Magnificent Desolation — The Long Journey Home From The Moon*, Harmony Books, 2009, p.89.
20. Ibid., p.86.
21. Cited, Osho, *The Great Zen Master Ta Hui*, Rebel Publishing, 1987, p.64.
22. Aldrin, *op. cit.*, pp.114–115.
23. Ibid., p.116.
24. Ibid., p.118.
25. Ibid., p.118.
26. Jung, quoted, Aldrin, ibid., pp.172–173.
27. Geoff Hurst, *1966 And All That — My Autobiography*, Headline Book Publishing, 2001, p.18.
28. David Cassidy, *Could It Be Forever — My Story*, Headline Publishing, ebook, 2007, pp.1899–1926.
29. Ibid., pp.1988–2001.
30. Ibid., p.1237.
31. Ibid., p.2028.
32. Nina Persson, 'The Cardigans were a machine' in *Independent*, 1 February 2009. https://www.independent.co.uk/arts-entertainment/music/features/nina-persson-the-cardigans-were-a-machine-1520051.html.
33. Cassidy, *op. cit.*, p.1278.
34. Ibid., p.1249.
35. Rebecca Nicholson, 'Emma Mackey: "You'd have to be a sociopath to want to be a celebrity"' in *The Guardian*, 5 January 2021. https://www.theguardian.com/film/2021/jan/05/emma-mackey-sex-education-disney-death-on-the-nile.
36. Cited, *The Limited Times*, 2 July 2021.

37. Newman, cited, Daniel O'Brien, *Paul Newman*, Faber and Faber, 2004, p.177.
38. Andrew Smith, 'Elastica limits' in *The Observer*, 10 March 2002.
39. Cassidy, *op. cit.*, p.1262.
40. Ibid., p.1443.
41. Ibid., p.1802.
42. Ibid., p.1880.
43. Ibid., p.2213.
44. Ibid., p.2354.
45. Ibid., p.2367.
46. Charles Darwin, *The autobiography of Charles Darwin, 1809–1882: with original omissions restored*, New York: Norton, 1969, p.139.
47. John Bowlby, *Charles Darwin – a biography*, Hutchinson, 1990, p.11.
48. Ibid., p.11.
49. Charles Darwin, *op. cit.*, p.139.
50. John Stuart Mill, *Autobiography of John Stuart Mill*, Columbia University Press, 1960, p.93.
51. Ibid., p.94.
52. Ibid.
53. Coleridge, cited, Mill, ibid., p.94.
54. Ibid., p.101.
55. Ibid., p.104.
56. Richard Dawkins, *The Selfish Gene*, preface to 1976 edition, Oxford University Press, 1989, p.v.
57. 'Noam Chomsky on Life & Love: Still Going at 86, Renowned Dissident is Newly Married,' *Democracy Now!*, YouTube, 3 March 2015. https://www.youtube.com/watch?v=ZLBXIujfMvE.
58. Erich Fromm, *On Being Human*, Continuum, 1997, pp.101–2.
59. Noam Chomsky, *Chronicles of Dissent – Interviews with David Barsamian*, AK Press, 1992, p.158.

60. Rutger Bregman, *Humankind – A Hopeful History*, Bloomsbury, 2019, p.245.
61. Noam Chomsky, *Chronicles of Dissent – Interviews with David Barsamian*, AK Press, 1992, p.238.
62. Ibid., p.248.
63. Merriam-Webster online dictionary. https://www.merriam-webster.com/dictionary/navel-gazing.
64. Fromm, *To Have Or To Be*, Abacus, 1978, p.147.
65. Ibid., p.147; my emphasis.
66. Maugham, *A Writer's Notebook*, Penguin, 1993, p.291.
67. Laura Archera Huxley, *You Are Not The Target*, Avon Books, 1963, p.5.
68. Rousseau, quoted, John Hope Mason, *The Indispensable Rousseau*, Quartet Books, 1979, p.20.
69. Hume, quoted, ibid., p.5.
70. Ibid., p.35.
71. Rousseau, quoted, ibid., pp.188–9; my emphasis.
72. Jean-Jacques Rousseau, *Reveries of The Solitary Walker*, Penguin Classics, 1979, p.88.
73. Rousseau, ibid., p.88; my emphasis.
74. Rabindranath Tagore, *The Complete Poetical Works of Rabindranath Tagore*, ebook version, ?e-artnow, 2020, p.419.

Note from the author

Thanks for reading *A Short Book About Ego ... and the Remedy of Meditation*. I hope you enjoyed it and will experiment with the remedy if you haven't already. You can visit the *Media Lens* website I co-edit here: www.medialens.org; and can contact me here: davidmedialens@gmail.com.

David Edwards was born in Maidstone, Kent, in 1962. After taking a degree in Politics at the University of Leicester, he worked in sales and marketing management for several large corporations. In 1991, he left the business world to concentrate on writing. He published *Free to be Human* (Green Books, 1995) and *The Compassionate Revolution* (Green Books, 1998), before co-founding the website, *Media Lens*, in 2001. In 2007, *Media Lens* was awarded the Gandhi Foundation's International Peace Prize. He is co-author (with David Cromwell) of three books: *Guardians of Power* (Pluto Press, 2006), *Newspeak in the 21st Century* (Pluto Press, 2009) and *Propaganda Blitz* (Pluto Press, 2018). He had a bi-weekly column in *Gulf Today* newspaper for five years, a monthly box column in the *New Statesman* for two years, and has been published in many newspapers and magazines.

Bibliography

Adams, Robert, *Silence of the Heart — Dialogues With Robert Adams*, Acropolis Books, 1999.

Aldrin, Buzz, *Magnificent Desolation — The Long Journey Home From The Moon*, Harmony Books, 2009.

Archera Huxley, Laura, *You Are Not The Target*, Avon Books, 1963.

Aronson, Harvey B., *Buddhist Practice on Western Ground*, Shambhala, 2004.

Baldwin, Arthur W., *Hector The Helicopter*, Reed International Books, 1964.

Beder, Sharon, *Global Spin — The Corporate Assault on Environmentalism*, Green Books, 1997.

Betts, Torben, *Muswell Hill*, Oberon Books, 2012.

Bloom, Alfred (ed.), *The Shin Buddhist Classical Tradition Volume 2: A Reader in Pure Land Teaching*, World Wisdom, 2014.

Bly, Robert (trans.), *The Kabir Book: Forty-Four of the Ecstatic Poems of Kabir*, Beacon Press, 1977.

Bowlby, John, *Charles Darwin — a biography*, Hutchinson, 1990.

Bregman, Rutger, *Humankind — A Hopeful History*, Bloomsbury, 2019.

Campbell, Joseph with Bill Moyers, *The Power of Myth*, Doubleday, 1988.

Cassidy, David, *Could It Be Forever — My Story*, Headline Publishing, ebook, 2007.

Chomsky, Noam, *Chronicles of Dissent — Interviews with David Barsamian*, AK Press, 1992.

Chomsky, Noam, *Deterring Democracy*, Hill and Wang, 1992.

Cutler, Howard, *The Art of Happiness*, Easton Press, 1998.

Darwin, Charles, *The Autobiography of Charles Darwin, 1809–1882*, Norton, 1969.

Dawkins, Richard, *The Selfish Gene,* Oxford University Press, 1989.

Durning, Alan, *How Much is Enough — The Consumer Society and the Future of the Earth,* Worldwatch Environmental Series, 1992.

Fromm, Erich, *On Being Human*, Continuum, 1997.

Fromm, Erich, *To Have Or To Be*, Abacus, 1978.

Gross, John (ed.), *The Oxford Book of Aphorisms,* Oxford University Press, 1983.

Hope Mason, John, *The Indispensable Rousseau,* Quartet Books, 1979.

Hurst, Geoff, *1966 And All That — My Autobiography,* Headline Book Publishing, 2001.

Kasser, Tim, *The High Price of Materialism,* The MIT Press, 2002.

Machiavelli, Niccolò, *The Prince,* Dover publications, 1992.

Marr, Andrew, *My Trade — A Short History of British Journalism,* Macmillan, 2004.

Maugham, Robin, *Conversations With Willie — Reflections of W. Somerset Maugham,* W.H. Allen, 1978.

Maugham, W. Somerset, *A Writer's Notebook,* Penguin, 1993.

Maugham, W. Somerset, *Collected Short Stories — Volume 1,* Penguin, 1984.

McEnroe, John, *Serious,* Hachette Digital, 2008.

Mill, John Stuart, *Autobiography of John Stuart Mill,* Columbia University Press, 1960.

Mill, John Stuart, *Utilitarianism,* Fount Paperbacks, 1979.

O'Brien, Daniel, *Paul Newman,* Faber and Faber, 2004.

Osho, *Dang Dang Doko Dang,* Osho Media International, 2015.

Osho, *Don't Just Do Something, Sit There,* Rebel Publishing, 1977.

Osho, *The Guest — Talks on Kabir,* Rajneesh Foundation, 1981.

Osho, *I Say Unto You, Volume 2 — Talks on the Sayings of Jesus,* Diamond Pocket Books, 2000.

Osho, *The Path of Paradox, Volume 1,* Osho International Foundation, 1981.

Osho, *The Revolution*, Rebel Publishing, 2000.

Osho, *Yoga — The Alpha and the Omega, Volume 7*, Rajneesh Foundation, 1977.

Rocker, Rudolf, *Culture and Nationalism*, Michael E. Coughlan, 1978.

Rousseau, Jean-Jacques, *Reveries of The Solitary Walker*, Penguin Classics, 1979.

Simpson, Joe, *Touching The Void*, Vintage, 1988.

Singer, Michael, *The Untethered Soul — The Journey Beyond Yourself*, New Harbinger, 2007.

Tagore, Rabindranath, *The Complete Poetical Works of Rabindranath Tagore*, e-artnow, 2020.

Taylor, Steve, *Extraordinary Awakenings — When Trauma Leads To Transformation*, New World Library, 2021.

Tolle, Eckhart, *The Power of Now*, Hodder & Stoughton, 2001.

Tolstoy, Leo, *Writings on Civil Disobedience and Non-Violence*, New Society, 1987.

Zopa Rinpoche, Lama, *Transforming Problems*, Wisdom Books, 1993.

Zopa Rinpoche, Lama, *Ultimate Healing*, Wisdom Books, 2001.

EASTERN RELIGION & PHILOSOPHY

We publish books on Eastern religions and philosophies. Books that aim to inform and explore the various traditions that began in the East and have migrated West.
If you have enjoyed this book, why not tell other readers by posting a review on your preferred book site.

Recent bestsellers from MANTRA BOOKS are:

The Way Things Are

A Living Approach to Buddhism

Lama Ole Nydahl

An introduction to the teachings of the Buddha, and how to make use of these teachings in everyday life.

Paperback: 978-1-84694-042-2 ebook: 978-1-78099-845-9

Back to the Truth

5000 Years of Advaita

Dennis Waite

A demystifying guide to Advaita for both those new to, and those familiar with this ancient, non-dualist philosophy from India.

Paperback: 978-1-90504-761-1 ebook: 978-184694-624-0

Shinto: A celebration of Life

Aidan Rankin

Introducing a gentle but powerful spiritual pathway reconnecting humanity with Great Nature and affirming all aspects of life.

Paperback: 978-1-84694-438-3 ebook: 978-1-84694-738-4

In the Light of Meditation

Mike George

A comprehensive introduction to the practice of meditation and the spiritual principles behind it. A 10 lesson meditation programme with CD and internet support.

Paperback: 978-1-90381-661-5

A Path of Joy

Popping into Freedom

Paramananda Ishaya

A simple and joyful path to spiritual enlightenment.

Paperback: 978-1-78279-323-6 ebook: 978-1-78279-322-9

The Less Dust the More Trust

Participating in The Shamatha Project, Meditation and Science Adeline van Waning, MD PhD

The inside-story of a woman participating in frontline meditation research, exploring the interfaces of mind-practice, science and psychology.

Paperback: 978-1-78099-948-7 ebook: 978-1-78279-657-2

I Know How To Live, I Know How To Die

The Teachings of Dadi Janki: A warm, radical, and life-affirming view of who we are, where we come from, and what time is calling us to do

Neville Hodgkinson

Life and death are explored in the context of frontier science and deep soul awareness.

Paperback: 978-1-78535-013-9 ebook: 978-1-78535-014-6

Living Jainism

An Ethical Science

Aidan Rankin, Kanti V. Mardia

A radical new perspective on science rooted in intuitive awareness and deductive reasoning.

Paperback: 978-1-78099-912-8 ebook: 978-1-78099-911-1

Ordinary Women, Extraordinary Wisdom

The Feminine Face of Awakening

Rita Marie Robinson

A collection of intimate conversations with female spiritual teachers who live like ordinary women, but are engaged with their true natures.

Paperback: 978-1-84694-068-2 ebook: 978-1-78099-908-1

The Way of Nothing
Nothing in the Way
Paramananda Ishaya
A fresh and light-hearted exploration of the amazing reality of nothingness.
Paperback: 978-1-78279-307-6 ebook: 978-1-78099-840-4

Readers of ebooks can buy or view any of these bestsellers by clicking on the live link in the title. Most titles are published in paperback and as an ebook. Paperbacks are available in traditional bookshops. Both print and ebook formats are available online.

Find more titles and sign up to our readers' newsletter at www.collectiveinkbooks.com/mind-body-spirit. Follow us on Facebook at facebook.com/OBooks and Twitter at twitter.com/obooks

PGIL2024USA